GW00399981

FISH OF THE SUMMER STILLWATERS

FISH OF THE SUMMER STILLWATERS

John Bailey

The Crowood Press

First published in 1991 by
The Crowood Press Ltd
Gipsy Lane, Swindon
Wiltshire SN2 6DQ

British Library Cataloguing in Publication Data

Bailey, John
Fish of the summer stillwaters
1. Angling
I. Title
799.12

ISBN 1 85223 403 2

Acknowledgements

I very gratefully acknowledge the help given to me by those great and generous anglers Shaun Harrison, Alan Rawden, John Sidley, Mick Brown and Brian Crawford.

Line-drawings by Chris Turnbull.

Typeset by MEP, Witney
Printed in Great Britain by
Redwood Press Ltd, Melksham, Wilts

Contents

Introduction

Everything began for me in the mid-1950s on the north-western canal system where I began to fish for roach with a plastic centrepin reel, a cane rod the thickness of a poker, a float Moby Dick would have had trouble sinking and hooks that might as well have been fashioned out of rubber. Still, I caught sticklebacks and then gudgeon and, as the pieces of the jigsaw fell into place, the occasional sprat-sized roach. From there I moved to bigger roach at Cheshire's Roman Lakes and then to perch at a small reservoir at Compstall, near Stockport. Soon I was to catch rudd at a certain Poynton Pool, crucian carp at Capesthorne Hall and then bream at Rudyard Lake and Tatton Mere.

Now it was the early 1960s and I was pursuing – and occasionally catching – tench at Norfolk's Holkham Lake and hideous, hypnotic eels at Selbrigg Pond. As teenage days developed, so did a passion for carp at Lyme Park in Cheshire, and then in the common ponds at Tooting and Clapham as student life was entered.

Finally, for many years of adulthood, I returned to Norfolk and rudd at Felbrigg Lake, tench at Wolterton Lake and to a hundred other pools, pits, ponds and lakes, where I have found peace, beauty and a great deal of wonderful fishing.

A perfect summer-caught roach

A fascination in ponds, however small.

You cannot start a child fishing too young!

In a nutshell, this is a condensed thirty years of bliss. I make it sound like a personal odyssey but, like any angler, I was helped continually along the way and my debt of thanks goes back and back.

In the beginnings, there was an ancient and frail grandmother who tottered with me along towpaths as knot tyer and lifeguard before I could swim. There were parents who drove me miles, often at dawn, to venues my bicycle would just not extend to. Bleary-eyed and tight-lipped, perhaps, but they never complained.

Then there was my early hero, canal ace Albert Oldfield, who would sit for hours behind me, prodding me on towards greater skills and understanding of the still water beneath me. I think around these days of the window cleaner who saw me in trouble and dropped his ladder down the high dam wall and netted for me my first two-pound roach. I thank, too, a northerner called Ron Bennett, who took me to the millponds at dawn and taught me the mystery of mists and tench.

Pete Warburton entered my life with a van and the petrol to take me into far-flung Cheshire and even down as far as Shropshire. He never let me down – though the van did often – and we began to catch serious fish. In London I met up with Dick Nichol, who offered much-needed partnership for those forays to Tooting Common, where the most sinister characters lurked after dusk. And, back in Norfolk, haven't my skills and enthusiasms over the years been encouraged by Johns Wilson, Judge and Nunn, by Joe Reed and finally, so importantly, by Roger Miller?

Dreaming of summer stillwaters?

If I were to calculate how many hours I have sat beside stillwaters with members of this gang or alone, it would truly frighten me. Tens of thousands of hours when I should have been studying or making money would seem wasted to the cynical non-angler. But then, I would have forgotten the lessons by now and spent the money and would not have had the deepest, richest store of waterside memories.

This book is obviously about catching stillwater species and I hope a fair bit will be learned from it. There are, however, stories entwined, tales of absolute passion and commitment which speak strongly for the hold this form of fishing can exert. Lakes are wonderful things, living eyes in the landscape, and it is impossible to imagine a fishing career without them. My advice is to go, to fish and, whether the catch be a four-ounce rudd or a forty-pound catfish, enjoy every precious minute.

The Basics

THE WATERS

The term 'summer stillwaters' provides a vast spectrum of fishing from the most enormous venues to the tiniest, from the most expected to the most bizarre and unusual. In my time I have fished reservoirs, pits, lakes, meres, broads, pools, moats, tiny marlpits, drainage ditches, coastal dykes and flashes, oxbow lakes, irrigation ponds, and even river-flooded abandoned swimming pools. Simply any dash of blue on a map needs investigation. Nothing can be written off until it has been vetted and even then, even after quite intensive fishing, I am always reluctant to write any water off completely.

The mystery of centuries – lilies, rudd, perch and eels inhabit the moat.

Carp observed.

To do so can be a mistake that is quite sickening: the summer I write this book (1990) I have had permission to tackle a delightful tree-shaded pool on the fringe of fenland. I gave it seven 12-hour sessions and registered a single, missed, bite. After this, I abandoned the pool only to be told two months afterwards of a 5lb 7oz crucian carp falling there.

Of course, most stillwaters are well advertised, well known, day-or season-ticket venues that need little or no discovery. Everybody knows about them and it is simply a question of finding a place in high season and extracting some fish of your own. But in many counties there are other opportunities.

The time to begin looking is early in May, when the weather picks up and there is the emergence of some hot weather. I personally follow any possible lead – a whisper on the grapevine, any scrap of blue on a map, simply driving and walking the valleys, dips and folds in a likely looking field. I always try to see a water and assess its potential before bothering with the frequently difficult process of seeking permission. On warmer days you may reasonably expect to see some trace of carp, rudd or bream and if your visit is at evening time then crucians and tench could well roll or bubble before you. There is also the chance of seeing some pike or perch activity. Sometimes there are waters that look perfect in every way but appear fishless. Perhaps they are, but more probably fish stocks are low and include large individual specimens.

To find the water is a major step but the owner still must be contacted. Generally his residence will be obvious. The nearby farmer or estate owner generally has rights but things can be more difficult in the case, say, of an old pit in scrubland. But then I go regularly until I chance upon someone on the banks or I ask at any nearby houses. Are letters, personal calls or telephone conversations the most profitable approach to an owner? After years of successes and rebuffs, I can catergorically state that the loser must be the telephone. The owner is probably tired, or eating, or expecting an important phone call, and you are simply an irritant and easily disposed of on the phone. There is no real contact and you have no chance to impress him with your obvious sincerity.

Equally, a premeditated personal call is dangerous; things can go horribly wrong. I remember a friend of mine calling at the door of an imposing stately home in the early evening, very smart and with a convincing tale upon his lips. He was met warmly by a gentleman in a dinner-jacket. 'So glad you are here,' he was told, and was then ushered into a bright warm room and given a small sherry. Before he himself could speak, he was instructed to sit down and 'we'll be down in a minute'. In the interim, the doorbell rang a second time and the

A well-kept Norfolk lake – the stagings will mellow in time and the willows crowd round.

proper taxi driver arrived! On that occasion the whole incident was treated with such humour and high spirits that my friend naturally got his permission. But you cannot rely on upper-class eccentricities all the time.

Safer, I am sure, is the very polite letter enclosing, of course, a stamped addressed envelope. This route at least virtually guarantees a reply from all but the rudest farmers. But, remember, the letter must be polite: you are asking a great favour and must not assume anything. Stress that you are a serious angler, that you never leave litter, that you care for wildlife, that you would obey any rules regarding parking, for example, and fishing times happily and without demur. Obviously, offer to pay a fee for this privilege – either to the owner himself or perhaps, as is popular, to his favourite charity. It is often a good idea to ask for only one, two or three days in the initial letter. Understandably, a lot of owners are worried about granting *carte blanche* permission but will listen to a more limited plea. Once you have been, have proved your worth and made personal contact, then the gates might be opened further.

This is how things once were, and still very often can be. But we do live in an increasingly commercial age. It is likely that the water you find will be syndicated, though you might still be offered the chance of a place. How much you should pay is up to your pocket and personal desire, but the inflated prices now being asked sadden me. Many landowners, probably being brought up in the salmon-fishing, pheasant-shooting scene, have a completely inflated idea of what their own small lake with its mediocre stock of coarse fish is worth. Yet, in these desperate days, they are often able to find a group of men willing to dig deep in the hope of finding a little paradise. This rarely happens.

The chances, of course, are improved if the group can take the water on a long lease. Then they can put into effect their own plans and shape the water much as they wish. It is vital, however, to insist on a long lease with the option to renew. Nobody wants to put in long hours of work and often expensive stock only to see it all lost to other anglers in a year or two's time. There are books on fishery management available so I will say no more except to add that it is a wise move, before signing, to call in a fishery expert such as Dr Bruno Broughton to give you his considered opinion on the water and its potential. It is very easy to be carried away by the romance of a pool and a little down-to-lakebed science is a useful investment.

Every season I take a fresh look at waters that I have known for years. Waters are highly dynamic environments and the fish stocks in them are rarely stable for long periods. All manner of influences affect them and fish of a quality that you would never expect to find there can quite suddenly appear. Often these are large public waters, fished for a pound or two, and you can have excellent sport that is unguessed at by many.

A boat has always been seen as an asset.

Finally, never dismiss the tiniest or whackiest of waters. I have already mentioned the decayed Edwardian swimming pool that provided me with a good-sized roach from the deep end. Recently I fished a Hungarian river. Wandering its banks, I came across a tiny pool ten yards from the river and obviously linked up in a winter flood. Now, though, it was quite separate and minute, only twenty yards by ten yards at the most. In it I saw, hooked and sadly lost a grass carp of, I would guess, between 25 and 30lb. Nothing can be overlooked.

READING THE WATERS

I can hardly remember a stillwater that has not rewarded the most painstaking observations and I truly believe that every hour spent researching more than pays for itself in fish caught. On large waters, I really need to get afloat – if the owner gives his permission. Being on the water gives a tremendous advantage and if there is a boat there or you own one yourself do make use of it. At the moment I am investigating the possibilities of Avon inflatable boats for the stillwater scene.

I like to get to the upwind end of the water and make several drifts down it, pushed along by the wind. There is little need to control the boat and I simply stand with polaroid glasses, scanning the water around me. In this way I have often seen quite unexpected fish, which will come close to the drifting, noiseless boat. I am happy to spend hours like this, watching, gradually piecing together a general impression of fish stocks and behaviour. My next step is to fasten on the fish finder. I use a Humminbird portable. It is light, reliable, and easy to operate and it gives a superb readout. If you do not own one, many tackle shops now hire them out for the day fairly cheaply. The value of finding every bar, every deep hole, every snag, every sunken weedbed and often deep-lying big fish cannot be overstated. Within a few hours even a big water can be thoroughly investigated. By now my confidence will be sky high. I know the fish, their habits and the water's geography. I can begin to make plans and to work out swims and ambush points.

The top end of Wolterton Lake . . . scene of Chris Turnbull's triumph.

Again the boat becomes vital. Now I can get right over the area I intend to fish and investigate it thoroughly. With an oar or a long pole I can scratch around the area, searching for the bottom make-up I like to fish over. I can pinpoint the harder areas of sand or gravel that many fish prefer to mud and silt. I can investigate thoroughly any snags and know just where the danger areas are. Rarely do I remove a snag, as this is probably the very feature that makes the swim so attractive in the first place. And lastly, from a boat, distance prebaiting can be carried out with the absolute precision that is impossible from the bank with catapult or throwing-stick.

If a boat is not available, and again if rules permit it, I will often swim out to make a thorough investigation of the swim area. I do choose a hot day for this before 16 June and I do like to have a friend with me just in case I do encounter difficulties. I also wear pumps as I swim, to avoid foot cuts on mussels, gravel bars, old bottles, ironware and the like. In short, I do swim with great care and consideration. Remember that things can go wrong and do not treat this type of preparation as a joke. Once in the water, you might be surprised how little afraid some species of fish are of the near-naked swimming angler. Many are almost welcoming in their attention. I first remember as a six-year-old swimming all afternoon in the company of a perch shoal, and similar things have happened many times since. Recently, in a Greek lake, a large common followed me for a hundred yards before shooting off – through boredom, I feel, rather than fear.

Small waters do not need these more elaborate approaches. Depth reading can be done adequately from the bank with rod, reel, float and lead. Fish-watching can be successful from trees, from behind bushes, from the tops of banks, with polaroid glasses and perhaps binoculars. A word here, perhaps, about the polaroids to buy. They are generally available with either grey or amber lenses. Personally I prefer the amber lenses as they seem to be able to put a little more light into the swim on the duller type of day. The really good makes such as the Cormorant series are expensive, I know, but the investment is a wise one. The frames last far longer and the lenses allow deeper water-penetration.

After spending this kind of money, it is foolish then not to obey two simple laws. Wear dull or even camouflaged clothing on the bankside and do move very slowly and carefully. Make use of every bit of cover available. I have found it never pays to stalk the water in a hurry. Patience is absolutely essential and I will sit happily in the sun watching one single lily-bed for two or three hours. Fish come and go and often something quite remarkable can emerge before you. A pool will not be hurried and you have to sink yourself into the slow-moving world of the water to get the ultimate rewards from it. To stop

Camouflage is all . . .

yourself fidgeting and shuffling it is wise to take along a cushion to make the bank that little bit more comfortable.

Hot, sunny weather is obviously ideal for getting to know a stillwater of any size and it seems that in the mid-afternoon the fish become particularly visible. Probably now the water is at its warmest and many fish are attracted to the surface. (Others, of course, head towards the cooler, darker deeps.) Around the turn of May and June it is possible that your trips will coincide with certain species on their spawning beds.

While the perfect swim differs according to the species sought, there is not a single fish that does not like a snag of some description. These are the landmarks of the water and they attract fish as surely as a wreck or a reef does in the sea. Most snags are obvious ones of fallen trees, but they can be as unusual as the discarded biscuit tin which became home to a two-pound perch of my acquaintance. Equally important are the bottom contours and the make-up of the bed itself. Deeper holes will attract crucians and common carp, especially if trees overhang. Plateaux will hold bream and rudd, while carp and tench will always follow the bars in a water.

. . . as is patience.

Roger Miller gets away from it all.

Wind direction plays its part in summer as surely as it does in winter. Perhaps in summer it is even more important, pumping much-needed oxygen and life into hot, increasingly stagnant waters. Open water in a small pool which attracts a ripple can be very productive. On bigger, more exposed waters the windward bank is usually favourite but it is essential to find the underwater currents as fish of all species will follow them. Casting around with an unfilled feeder will gradually teach you where to expect the strongest underwater pulls and pushes of water. Indeed, it is wrong to see stillwaters as 'still' at all when they are of even moderate size. On the biggest reservoirs a wind can set up an underwater flow that can move a 2oz bomb, and the effect is only gradually scaled down according to water size and wind strength. Certainly, many fish constantly reposition themselves according to these hidden currents and are probably more active than river fish of the same species.

Water-weed is a vital attraction to fish, all through the spring, summer and well into the winter. It provides shade, food, protection and oxygen, and swims well away from weed growth rarely produce the goods in a constant way. The only weed types that do not seem to be of real interest to fish are Canada weed and mares tail, but even these are sought out if there is nothing else in the water. Water-weeds are not to be despised but should be seen as the sign of a happy, healthy water and will help fish to find the sanctuary they

This Kashmir carp fisherman knows the value of weedbeds.

Weed that even ducks cannot get through!

so often need to get away from anglers. Weed can often become a dubious friend in a hot summer, especially when there is the light and the warmth to foster explosions of the stuff. Many times, waters have become virtually impossible to fish without some weed cutting. This, though, is not as easy as it may seem. The weed does not grow predictably like the lawn outside your house. Cutting weed might even spread the spores and encourage even faster growth. In certain conditions, some types can even grow back again at a foot or more every twelve hours. The message is obviously to cut weed with care and consideration.

Where it is essential, the best cutter I ever devised was an 18-inch iron bar with a loop soldered to the head and two 9-inch grass-cutting blades bolted to the bottom. I could throw the device ten yards or so and it sank like a stone and cropped the weed at the very root. This is my usual design but recently I have seen commercially available tools. Do not cut weed where and when you will annoy fellow anglers already fishing and please check through the weed before it is dumped. Frequently small fish will be harboured in the clumps and they deserve a better fate than slow suffocation. Also, do be careful taking the weed off the blades as it is very easy to slice your fingers badly. I have sometimes lost blood at such a rate that I feared that the whole pool would be reddened.

John Nunn checks the weed for tiny life . . . the weed-cutter lies at his feet.

WEATHER

Weather is vital to the fisherman's successes, both winter and summer. At least in the summer it can never be so extreme that it actually prevents you from fishing at all. Hot, still spells are probably the most difficult to come to terms with but fish will still feed even in the drought conditions such as those of of 1976 or 1990. Most obviously, the very hot, still conditions do favour floater fishing for carp and for rudd. Prolonged high temperatures seem to build up the layer of surface scum and more and more fish begin to look for food elsewhere. Fishing becomes patchy as the feeding spells decline.

A great many species begin to feed predominantly between early darkness and late dawn. In the hottest weather, the first hour of true darkness, for example, often sees roach, bream, crucians, carp and tench feed quite hard. It can become important to be the night owl in these periods, though surprises in the daytime are always quite possible. The largest eel I ever hooked, and sadly lost, fed at midday one steaming August. By stalking tench in the shallows one sweltering July spell, Chris Turnbull landed two 6lb-plus fish on freelined flake between the weedbeds.

Summer evening when the sun sets over the float and the swallows are out.

The type of weather when fish feed all day through.

The period when the heatwave begins to break down in thunderstorms is always promising, even in the late afternoon, when a lot of these storms seem to break. The sultry atmosphere followed by cascades of fresh water stimulates all the species of the stillwaters and the more violent the storm the better. I remember sitting on a lake which was beginning to flood and to turn the colour of chocolate and seeing the carp population go wildly on the feed. That evening I had four runs compared with just two in the previous ten days.

Unsettled weather in summer presents its own problems. The approach of a severe depression, in my experience, appears to put paid to sport more than any other weather factor I know of. Over the years, again and again, seemingly splendid mornings have been quite fruitless only to be followed by a cold front of wind and rain tracking over from the west. Sustained periods of cloud and light rain on the other hand, can be very productive, providing the wind carries very little chill in it. A warm, grey day with spasmodic drizzle and moderate breeze I find splendid for every species that inhabits the stillwaters. Bream and tench will feed day long and even more unreliable feeders such as eel, crucian carp and catfish will stay on the move long past usual rest periods. Some of the very best fishing I have ever experienced has fallen in the Indian summers that we enjoy in so many years. I first really took advantage of these periods during college days, when I worked the majority of the summer through and took September and early October off to fish. Generally, the warm weather lingered on and the nights never did more than hint at frost. I found that many of the waters really came on with a vengeance and I believed then that many

The traditional lake nestles in its valley.

fish were using this final summer burst to build up energy before the ravages of winter. I still feel this hypothesis to be a correct one, and certainly fishing for most of the so-called summer species can reach a peak in early October, up until the sharp change in the weather that generally occurs around the third week of that month.

Although this is not quite connected with the weather, I have recently become very interested in the effect of the new and full moon on angling. I feel a great deal more research is necessary on this subject. Once a month, the sun and moon are together in the sky. This creates a new moon. Around two weeks later, the moon is opposite the sun in the sky – the full moon. In the twentieth century we have lost our sense of connectedness with the natural rhythms of nature. We have lost our lunar consciousness, but in earlier days lunar influences were considerably more predominant than they are now. The Hebrew calendar, for example, is based upon thirteen lunar months. Certainly, the language of the calendars of many primitive cultures reflects the importance that the moon had for these peoples.

The point I wish to make is that with some very simple observation of the heavens we can perhaps improve our catches significantly. Scientists know a lot about the influence of new and full moon upon the earth and upon human and animal behaviour. The combined gravitational pull when both sun and moon are in alignment actually causes water to rise, fall and contract. Our electrical and chemical balance is altered and this leads to alterations in behaviour – more admissions to mental hospitals, more births, more sexual activity. Most importantly, fish tend to feed *en masse* for longer periods of time and are more easily caught by anglers. In Britain we are only just beginning to acknowledge these forces whereas on the Continent they are openly discussed. I recently discussed this with a German angler who was quite happy to state that he only fished for carp at times of full and new moon, and certainly his results seemed to bear out this confidence.

ACCESSORIES

Just as winter demands thermal boots and one-piece jackets, so summer fishing calls for specialized accessories which can be overlooked. It does not do to put the warm clothing permanently into storage. Summer nights can be very cold indeed and temperatures can dip alarmingly when the skies are clear and the moon is a big one. All regular summer night fishers know to take warm gear but a mere frost can catch out the angler giving a night session a first try. Those hot but wet days are also a problem for the angler who dislikes fishing under an umbrella. Fortunately, there are now on the market a number of very light waterproof jackets and suits which are excellent for letting internal moisture out and yet keeping the rain at bay.

It is warm, wet days such as these that attract the mosquitoes the most, and some low-lying marsh-surrounded lakes can become irritating, or hazardous, or even impossible to fish. Then, of course, there are those mild, windless nights when the trees round the bubbling tench pool seem to harbour every midge in the universe. For both, a really good insect repellent is essential. For several years now I have used Jungle Formula. If it can allow me to fish during the summer in Scotland then I am safe just about anywhere.

Nor should you neglect the effects of the sun, especially if you are on a week's eel or catfish session and even more so if this is taking place on a water somewhere in France or southern Europe. Sunburn can happen easily, quickly and unnoticed and quite ruin an otherwise well-planned expedition. Take a highly protective suncream or even a complete block cream for a sensitive nose. Spend the heat of the day under shade until you are used to it. I have seen anglers sick, dizzy and quite unable to fish effectively after 36 hours beside southern European lakes. Also be very careful about the effects of dehydration. Alcohol is not necessarily the best drink to have at your side in very hot temperatures. Far better to take mineral water or pop.

Camera work can be slightly more difficult in very strong lights. A polaroid filter tends to deepen colours that can otherwise become bleached out. Also beware of the over-use of a wide-angle lens that drags in a greater amount of light.

CARE OF THE FISH

It would be quite criminal if I did not mention the fish themselves. Very frequently the summer is the most stressful time for them to be caught. Low water levels, low oxygen counts, and post-spawning cuts and lesions all render fish less able to deal with the traumas of capture and especially confinement in keepnets. Certain rules, it seems to me, must be obeyed for the life, possibly, of often ageing important fish. This was brought home to me in the saddest

It pays to return tench to deeper water, where they can recover without danger from heron attack.

fashion in 1989. I was fishing on an estate lake in very hot conditions when I stuck into one of the very old wild carp that still inhabited the water. It fought well until ten yards from the net, when suddenly everything went solid and lifeless on me. I thought that the fish had weeded and escaped until I continued to reel in and found the carp still attached. It was quite dead. Its fins still twitched in death spasms. I can only assume that the heat and stress were too much for an old and tired fish and I blamed myself bitterly for some time. An equally tragic experience hit me hard in 1975. Joe Reed and I had put together an impressive haul of ten 2lb-plus rudd in the period up till midnight. We decided to keep them in the net till morning for photographs. After the photographic session many of the fish were very slow in getting away and later in the week I saw three dead in the margins. Perhaps more died unseen out in the lake, but even 30 per cent is a terribly high mortality rate and I've been careful not to keep rudd in nets since.

The same must be said for bream. Bream are a bulky yet delicate fish and they suffer a very great deal in the net. The mesh rubs away their slime quickly and serious haemorrhaging rapidly follows. A clutch of big bream held for

How many did die that had been left that night?

A very young John Bailey, who failed to appreciate eels then for their natural history and mystery.

any length of time in a keepnet soon begin to look a sad, sorry and potentially deathly sight. Sack a large one if you must but let the others go as they are caught, please. This must be the message to any serious angler who is after any of the summer species in still or running water.

For the survival of many a big eel over the last fifteen years or so we must all thank John Sidley. His 'Put Eels Back' campaign has reached thousands of anglers in the 1970s, 80s and 90s, even people like me who up until 1974 were quite happy to catch an eel, take it and donate it to the pot. Then, obviously, I was as ignorant of the eel's potential age and romantic life cycle as anyone else.

THE MESMERIC CATFISH

Catfishing in Britain at the start of the 1990s is not totally unlike the carp-fishing situation at the start of the 1960s or even the 1950s. The fact is that there are still very few catfish waters and cats therefore possess an exciting rarity value. Most anglers have never even seen one and that alone lends them an element of the exotic. Add to this the cat's size, looks and fighting ability and the scope for rumour, mystery and legend is enormous. There cannot be any serious angler who is not fired by the thought of an unknown catfish water near him and anglers have embarked on the craziest of campaigns in pursuit of a dream, of a fantasy. Notable was the effort put in on Wilstone Reservoir (still holder of the cat record though a cat has not been recorded there for years and years) by a team in the 1980s who spent weeks baiting with rabbit and offal for not a single run. Still, nobody laughed at them. Had they been successful it would have been the angling coup of the decade. Who would have wanted to be seen scoffing at that?

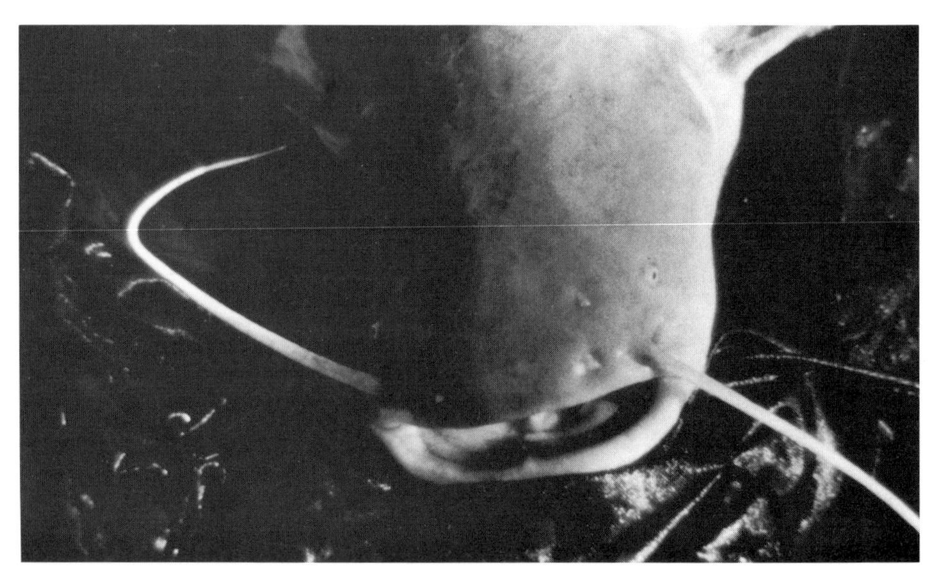

The sensivity of the cat's whiskers is extraordinary.

East Anglia is not a stronghold of catfish by any stretch of the imagination but even here cat mania struck – ignited largely by the amazing capture of a good-sized fish from the vast and wild waters of the upper Thurne region. How that cat got there is anybody's guess but it spawned a whole host of rumours – one being that the boat dykes were so full of the things it would hardly be wise to dip a toe overboard. One account I still like to give some credit to is a story of a cat found comatose in a boat dyke during a cold winter snap. Rumour was that the five-foot giant was lifted from the water on an oar before it slipped off and waddled slowly and sleepily away.

There were also tales of fish in the Ouse, of monsters having been seen rolling beneath road bridges. Yet, strangely, I was never able to find any record of a man landing one or, come to that, even fishing for one. Mind you, would I have ever had the courage to ledger some vast bait for a species of fish conspicuous only, probably, by its complete and utter absence?

I have, however, seen an East Anglian catfish, the first I have ever actually clapped eyes on. It was caught by Martyn Page and I had the unenviable task of landing it. After he had spent weeks in its pursuit and had to wade half the length of the lake to get it to the net, I hardly felt like bodging it for him then. Suffice it to say that I had a massive respect for the species from that evening, especially after seeing the fish motionless on the grass. I have not seen such resignation to fate in the eyes of any living creature since leaving the villages of the North Indian plains.

Since that night I have had some meetings with catfish abroad, including a 'thing' between five and six hundred pounds. Quite how such a creature could be landed without injury either to it or to me I did not know. However, I did stroke it – with a deal more circumspection than I would show the average moggy – and was not altogether sorry to see the line cut and the creature disappear at last beneath the boat. Fortunately, I doubt whether English cats will ever reach fifteen feet in length – though, as Shaun Harrison knows, they can be very formidable indeed.

The Obsession

Shaun Harrison

I first fished for catfish in 1984 in between carp trips. The first venue I fished was Claydon Lakes in Buckinghamshire. That first visit was like walking around a Who's Who of specimen-hunting waxworks, with anglers such as Dave Plummer, Chris Turnbull, Andy Barker, Kevin Maddocks, Vic Gillings and the ever-cheerful Phil Smith present.

I caught a few cats that first year but nothing very spectacular. At the time I was catching a lot of carp elsewhere and succeeded in breaking the carp record on three different lakes in the process. So, with one thing and another, I never really came to grips with the cats. My main problem at the time was missing runs. This was purely down to my lack of knowledge of the species and after a dozen or so trips I decided to knock it on the head as I was doing

To Shaun, a lovely sight.

so well carping at the time and didn't feel as though I could devote enough time to the cats.

The cats were forgotten about for the remainder of that season and during the following year I continued to catch plenty of carp, upping my personal best several times. The catfish had been forgotten about until the phone rang in August 1986. It was my mate Graham Slater, with whom I had fished on our very first catfish expedition. He had just returned from Claydon after hammering the cats on a new bait, mackerel. I forget now but I think he had caught about twenty fish, with the largest going 18–19lb. These were all caught during a duff period when very few other fish were coming out. Obviously, he had done a few things differently from the other anglers present. The main reasons for his success were: he didn't use a hair rig (everyone else did at the time); he had a different bait to offer them; and he baited up heavily whereas most others were relying on hook baits only. At this time I was struggling on a very hard carp syndicate water so when I was asked if I fancied another go at the cats I jumped at the chance. I had already got a couple of days booked off work the following week so we made arrangements.

The first two days were very unproductive, with very few fish of any species being caught. There were also a lot of anglers present, a fact that at the time I thought – wrongly – was the main reason for the lack of action. The inactivity continued until the third evening, when suddenly the whole lake switched on. It was absolutely incredible. I have still never seen last knockings to match it. (You can't night fish at Claydon). All around there were buzzers screaming, clutches screaming and anglers screaming. Everyone seemed to be playing a cat. That is, apart from just three people. Yes, you've guessed it – Graham, Paul Carter and myself. I had resigned myself to the fact that I was going to have a glorious blank when suddenly my buzzer came to life as the bobbin slid off the needle.

My immediate reaction instead of striking was to look to my right at someone who was playing a fish. I had taken it for granted that his fish had picked up one of my lines. It wasn't until I saw his fish netted and my line still pouring off the spool that I realized that I had a run.

I shut the bail arm and whacked into what was obviously a decent fish. After the usual brilliant fight Graham netted a 20lb 14oz cat for me. Obviously, I was absolutely thrilled. What a welcome back after such a lay-off from catting! I did, however, feel a little guilty about Graham because after his success the previous week he deserved the twenty far more than I did. All I had done was to cast out and wind it in. It had been all Graham's thinking behind the capture, the bait and the rig. Unfortunately, after I had caught this fish Graham lost interest and turned his attention to zander.

After a couple more hard carp sessions I couldn't resist another crack at the cats. My next trip was another three-day affair. I caught nothing. I returned home, worked for a day, then drove the ninety miles back for another go, this time accompanied by Bazz Tyson for his first attempt at a Claydon cat. We fished all day and still caught nothing. Nothing else was being caught but I wasn't happy. Graham had done well but everyone else had jumped on the bandwagon so almost every bait cast into Claydon now looked, smelled and behaved the same way. A new approach was obviously already called for.

The following day at work I juggled around in my mind various ideas. I found it hard as I had so little catfishing experience to relate to. One thing I had noticed on previous trips was the occasional appearance of oil slicks on the surface. This I put down to the release of oil from the mackerel as it was being crushed by the cats' teeth. As most people were baiting up at this stage it seemed obvious that the fish were swimming around and just picking up the odd bait rather than getting their heads down and feeding heavily, as they had on Graham's bait.

Three days later and I was back on a single Sunday session. This time I fished one rod to a solitary double half-mackerel and the other to sand eel. This I fished over a carpet of chopped sand eels. At the time I didn't know of anyone else who had used sand eel so I was confident of that one going. By mid-afternoon nothing had been caught, though I had noticed the occasional oil patch appearing around the lake. Never once did a large slick appear or two slicks together. It was now obvious to me that most of the cats were unwilling to say in one area and feed.

At 6 p.m. I had six anglers in my pitch. We were all sitting there putting the world to rights when by bobbin slowly crept up the needle. I looked out into the lake and saw a slick over my solitary bait. I struck into it and found myself playing a very irate cat. It charged about all over the lake while a party of American sightseers gathered round to watch the show.

When I finally got it on to the bank the Americans thought it was repulsive and wouldn't stand anywhere near it. The cat obviously thought that they were repulsive as well because it wouldn't stop grunting. Now, for anyone who hasn't seen a catfish, I had better explain that the occasional one makes some very strange noises, quite loud at times, too. Anyway, this fish weighed 18lb 6oz. Obviously, I was pretty pleased as I felt I deserved a little more than twenty. I had caught it after a little thought instead of copying someone else. If I remember right, my fish was the only one caught that day.

After this I started to put a lot more time in after the cats. The last hour of the day seemed to produce the most fish so by having two separate days off work a week I was able to fit in four last hours. For example, I would finish

Shaun and a brace of giants.

work at 6 p.m. on the Tuesday evening, drive the ninety miles to the lake, fish the last hour (remember that you can't night fish at Claydon). Sleep in the car park, then fish all day until the magical last knockings on the Wednesday. I would then do the same on the Saturday evening and Sunday. By the middle of September, with the nights drawing in, I was no longer able to make it to the lake in the time, so I had to put up with only two days a week. However, now that I was beginning to learn a little more about cats I was managing to coax a few out in the daytime.

It was about this time that I started to play around with flavoured baits. After a number of unsuccessful combinations I finally sorted out two that worked really well. One of these combinations consisted of Catchum's blended fish oil, standard Sense Appeal and emulsifier. This I would mix up at home in a bucket, soak my baits in it overnight and then take them to the lake in a polythene bag. The first week that I used this combination I really did business, catching four cats of over twenty pounds. These were in cold water conditions. In fact there had been frosts at the beginning of the week and these were the only cats caught that week, despite quite a number of anglers being present.

By this stage I was managing to catch cats on almost every trip while most others were struggling. There were now quite a lot of things that I was doing differently but I suppose the most important of them was hitting twitchers. Out of the four twenties that I have just mentioned only one gave a proper run.

For the previous couple of weeks we were all having trouble with what we thought were carp and bream taking the baits. Now, because the cats were going well on my baits, I was loath to change them. The only way I could think of scaring the carp and bream off my baits was to try and catch a few of them. For this reason I set up with a much smaller piece of bait and sat tight to the rods. I started to get twitches again and the first one I managed to hook turned out to be a 20lb-plus cat. By using the small baits I did start to catch quite a number of carp and bream. These didn't really annoy me much as I was still catching a couple of cats most days. Besides, the bream and carp were helping to keep me alert enough to hook the cats.

By October I was really beginning to sort them out and had decided to carry on through the winter since I felt it would only be a matter of time before a really big one came along. I then had a bad car crash and had to scrap all thoughts of winter catting. With my car off the road I didn't fancy a 180-mile walk twice a week!

THE 1987–88 SEASON

The new season started typically cold, wet and windy. What ever happened to those calm, misty early-season dawns that Mr Crabtree used to fish in?

During the close season I had decided to spend all my spare time fishing for the cats. I wanted to catch one fish in particular, and that was the big brown one that lives in Claydon. Now this fish is an amazing creature. Apart from being by far the biggest in the lake, for some reason it seems to be able to avoid capture. On one occasion it managed to go four years without a visit to the bank. That may not sound too much out of the ordinary until you consider that from 16 June until the end of September nearly every swim on the lake is occupied every day. There used to be three other cats weighing 28lb-plus, occasionally pushing 30lb, in Claydon. However, I am now sure that they are no longer there, though I would love to be proved wrong. These fish were known as Spot (on the dorsal), Warts (on the feeler), and Scarface (which speaks for itself). Does anyone reading this feel guilty about their disappearance?

Obviously, if I were going to stand a chance of catching the brown one I would have to tackle him differently without making it too obvious what I was doing. I feared other anglers jumping on the bandwagon and ruining my fishing as they had Graham's the year before.

During the close season I spent hours scouring the supermarket shelves, fish stalls, and butchers trying to find something completely different to use as bait. The previous four most successful baits used at Claydon had been, in order, squid, live fish, eel sections and mackerel. The squid and eel sections had 'blown' unless flavoured and the mackerel was slowly coming to join them. Obviously, I wanted to find something as different from those baits as possible. Unfortunately, the only things that I found would, I was sure, get me into trouble with the bream and carp. This had to be one of the major considerations as they seemed to devour just about anything that they could get in their mouths and not give the cats chance to find it. In fact the previous season I had been catching both carp and bream on half mackerel tails.

One of the baits I had seriously thought about was large flat boilies. They would flutter down and rest lightly on top of the disgusting black silt that covers the bottom. Boilies had accounted for some big cats in the past but, considering the amounts put into the lake by the carp anglers, very few were actually caught on them.

The season was about to start and I still hadn't sorted out any different baits. Until, that is, I decided to make some sausages – but without the sausage meat. This opened up a whole new area of bait. I could make them smell and sink exactly as I wanted, and I could make them just as tough as I wanted, with almost any type of texture. In other words, I had at my disposal what I considered to be the ideal bait. So simple, yet I hadn't previously thought of using this type of bait.

Finally – after revisiting the fish stalls, the butchers, and the hospitals – I found what I was looking for. I decided on two types; one would be meat-based and the other, fish-based. I also decided to carry on with the doctored mackerel as a standby as long as they were still taking it.

The season started wet, cold and windy. On my first day back I managed to catch a 14lb 14oz cat. Only two others were caught, though I annoyingly managed to miss three unmissable takes that I am sure were from cats. These first three takes I had struck at immediately, as had been best the previous season. On the fourth run I delayed the strike for a few seconds and this was the one that I connected with. During the next couple of weeks it soon became apparent that by delaying the strike I was hooking a bigger proportion of the takes than I was by hitting them immediately. To prevent me from striking I started to sit a little farther back from the rods than normal. All the fish that I caught were hooked perfectly in the corner of their mouths.

By the 3 July I had caught several doubles, including two twenties. My twentieth cat of the season came on 8 July. Obviously my methods and baits were going really well, as I didn't know of anyone else who had caught even half that amount.

A quick note on my methods at that time. I was freelining with 6-foot-long braided-nylon hooklinks. There was a reason for the length. All the other anglers that I saw freelining were using comparatively short hooklinks, down to about 8 inches at times. I reasoned, though, that because catfish don't have any scales it would be easy for them to detect the stiff nylon line against their bodies (I was using 11lb). For that reason I used the soft braided hooklinks long enough to almost eliminate the possibility of the fish coming into contact with the nylon.

A size 4 chemically sharpened hook was attached to one end and a Drennan ring to the other to cut down the resistance of a swivel. I had learned the previous season how important it was to minimize the resistance. Because of this fact I used extremely light bobbins in conjunction with Optonics. On windy days, to prevent the buzzers from constantly bleeping, I decided that I could simply switch them off rather than put on heavier indicators. In calm conditions, on the other hand, I would very often do away with the bobbins altogether and simply place the rod on an Optonic with the bail arm off and watch the line at the rod tip.

Another thing I learned was that during hard times the fish didn't like having baits cast on their heads. The way I overcame this problem (so long as there was no one opposite me) was to PVA a piece of dry mud or stone to the bait, cast it to the far margin and then slowly edge it back into the swim. This way I very often got a take straight after manoeuvring the bait into the swim, – whereas if I cast and left the bait where it landed most takes would come only after it had been out for a while.

The day I caught my twentieth of the season was a very memorable one for several reasons, both good and bad. It all started on the motorway on the Tuesday evening. I was just approaching the Watford Gap services when there was a loud knock in my engine, the battery light came on and the temperature gauge shot up. It seemed obvious that the fanbelt had snapped, so without bothering to look under the bonnet I cruised into the services and rang the RAC for assistance as I didn't have a spare with me. The usual 45 minutes passed and the breakdown wagon duly arrived. I then opened the bonnet for the first time and immediately noticed a gap where there shouldn't have been one. Then it suddenly dawned on me. The loud knock had been the alternator falling off. The RAC man had a fanbelt but no alternator to attach it to. As I am in the Relay service he told me that he would have to tow me home and leave me to sort it out there. I didn't seem to have a great deal of choice. I was going to miss an evening and a day catting. Or was I?

A quick bit of thinking got me back on my way to the lake. I told the RAC man that I had recently moved from Nottingham down to Buckingham and hadn't yet got round to changing the address on my card. As my signature matched up he had no reason to disbelieve me. The things I do for a day's fishing! Anyway, I was soon being chauffeur-driven to the lake with my van strapped up on the back. I glanced at my watch and reasoned that if my chauffeur speeded things up a little I would still get the last thirty minutes fishing in. So lie number two was told to the kind, trusting RAC man. I forgot what I told him but whatever it was worked as he started to put his foot down a little more and we arrived at the car park on time. I had to lie to him a third time and tell him that I lived in the big stately home in the field. I think he possibly began to doubt my honesty at this stage as it would be unlikely that I would be driving about in an old van if I lived in a place like that. After many thank-yous I ran across the field armed with two rods, a landing net, camera, scales and a pocket full of smelly bait.

I cast out my two baits and was on my way for a chinwag with Vic Gillings and Dylan and Simon Wrathall when my buzzer sounded. I rushed back and whacked into a catfish. After a short hectic fight I landed a kitten of about 8lb. I had just removed the hook when the second buzzer sounded. I rushed the first fish back to the water and struck into the second. It was immediately obvious that this was a big one. I was up at the shallow end and the fish slowly took line until it reached the other bank and ran out of water. It then moved up the far margin for about thirty yards before getting bored and swimming back to me. I thought I was pulling it back until it came level and just carried on swimming past me with the rod wrapped right round. It ran another ten yards, totally unimpressed, turned, shook its great head under the water, sending the water black with mud, and then the rod sprang back. I thought at first that it had bitten through the braided line as I had had that happen once before during the previous season with a big one, but on inspection I found I had merely pulled out. Anyway, it was time to leave for the Crown Inn at Steeple Claydon for a pint. If you ever fish at Claydon, you will soon realize that it is essential to visit the Crown. We only go for two reasons. If we catch anything resembling a catfish (a gudgeon will do at a push) we go to celebrate and if we don't catch anything we go to drown our sorrows.

Because of the large number of cats that I was catching I was starting to get pressure from other people to have a go at another water which is known to contain some very large cats of still unknown size. Now, although I had caught a lot of fish at Claydon, I still hadn't had the one that I had set my heart on. No one else had caught it either so as I had caught more than twice as many as the next person that season I felt that I stood a good chance of hooking it. I decided to persevere, despite having recaptured several of the bigger ones. Little did I know that my turn was soon to come.

Once again I raced down the motorway to fit in the last 30 minutes' fishing. The nights were once again beginning to draw in and I was having difficulty getting down in time, so because of this I decided to buy a new, faster van. I caught nothing on that particular Saturday evening, though I managed to miss one. We had a good night that night. After visiting the Crown for the usual pint and meal we went back to the car park armed with some takeouts and had a party round my van to the sound of T-Rex. In the early hours we all retired to our motors for some much-needed sleep.

The following day down at the lake the weather was miserable. It was windy, wet and cold. To top it all the water temperature was well down. With the weather how it was there wasn't much chance of the water temperature rising. In an attempt to cheer ourselves up we decided to hold a Claydon Olympics. We had various competitions, including welly throwing and Claydon's strongest man. This involved holding a freezer box of bait out at arms length for as long as possible without bending the arm. I got a joint first in this event so I at least had a result in the morning. At dinner we decided that it was time to settle down to some serious fishing. During the morning we had had no trouble with bream or carp taking the baits. Because of this I decided to put some really small baits on. I concluded that I would stand a better chance of tempting a cat in the cold water with a small bait rather than one of conventional size.

I wound a rod in and recast with a small running lead and a paternoster link to help keep the ledger bead out of the silt to avoid too much resistance. I recast with a bait the size of my thumbnail. Shortly afterwards I missed a fast take. I recast and settled back. My Optonic sounded again. I struck immediately but felt nothing. I wound down quickly and the rod started to bend. After taking the bait the fish had obviously swum straight towards me. Upon proper contact the fish turned round and swam to the other bank, then started to swim down the lake to the right. It had kept in the far margin and swum by about six swims before stopping and waving its tail in the air. It was too far away for me to see how big it was as I had stood my ground to play it instead of following it down the lake. It fought very powerfully, making several slow but unstoppable runs. After fifteen minutes the closest I had managed to get it back was two swims away. By now I had eight people in my swim eager to know what I had hooked this time. Eventually I got it to about three rod-lengths out but still couldn't lift it to the surface for a look. The water was only about two feet deep in this part so it was obvious that I was well stuck into something a little larger than normal. There were huge patches of black mud rising to the surface as the fish tried hard to bury itself in the thick silt.

I asked Brian Smalley if he would do the honours with the net as he was by far the most experienced at netting big cats. There were three different conversations going on at the time. I turned around and said jokingly that it was probably a little kitten foul-hooked. Suddenly a huge head lifted out of the water and Brian calmly stated the obvious:

'You've got it at last, its the big brown one.'

Big wasn't the word. It looked bloody enormous to me.

I started to worry about the small hook; I had only put on a size 8 because of the tiny bait that I was using. I didn't know if it would take the strain of such a large fish at the netting stage, as cats have to be half lifted out of the

A cat at last light.

water in order to get their long bodies into the landing net. Anyway, the next time I had it on the surface it was at the net. I heaved its head over the drawcord and up to the spreader block but half of it was still hanging out of the net. Brian scooped but it didn't fold in. He flipped the net a second time and got the fish three-quarters in. The third time that he shook the net it finally folded into the mesh. Yet it still wasn't all over. The fish rose like a great serpent on its tail in the shallow water and was half out the net again. Brian scooped quickly before it had a chance to leave the net completely and this time, on the second scoop, it was right in, beaten at last. Suddenly there was a big cheer from behind. This was the first sound from my audience since the great smiling head had lifted out of the water the first time during the fight. Brian carefully laid it out on the bank and it looked truly enormous. After a lot of effort and expense I had finally cracked it. The size 8 hook was firmly tucked into the corner of its huge mouth. Now came the weighing. I wetted the huge weigh sling and it was just as I had expected, the Avons were pulled to their limit well before the fish was getting anywhere near off the ground.

The fish was retained in the water for a short time while I went back to the van for my big scales. The needle finally settled down at a fraction under 35lb. I decided to settle for 34lb 12oz to save any unnecessary argument. Although I probably did myself out of a couple of ounces, I wasn't bothered in the slightest.

After returning the fish alive to the water I sat back and thought of the many, often lonely, hours I had spent fishing for that one fish before I finally caught it at its biggest weight ever. At the time of capture it is the largest catfish caught in this country by an angler fishing for them. The record is held by an angler who was pike fishing, caught by accident from a water that hadn't previously produced a catfish. Unfortunately, this fish died on its way to a zoo so there was never any chance of a repeat capture.

The Story of the Catfish in Britain

Shaun Harrison

This chapter draws on a collection of literature that I have gathered over the years on the Danubian wels (*Siluris glanis*), more commonly known as the catfish. My purpose is to let a few more people know how catfish came into this country as I am constantly surprised by the number of customers who come into the tackle shop where I work and confess that they don't realize that we have such things swimming around our lakes.

It all began on 27 October 1880, when Britain received its first shipment of wels. The man responsible for this was Lord Odo Russell, a member of the famous Russell family of Woburn Abbey. He was, incidentally, also responsible for the introduction of the grey squirrel into this country.

The first shipment of seventy catfish was transported from a fish farm in Germany and put into the lakes at Woburn Abbey, after which these fish were more or less left to their own devices. Woburn Abbey was strictly out of bounds to most anglers, so the original stocking was left to grow unhindered.

In 1907 a second batch of catfish was brought into the country, this time by a member of the wealthy Rothschild family, and these fish were stocked into Marsworth Reservoir, near Tring. Tring Reservoirs were constructed in the nineteenth century for the purpose of holding water to top up the Grand Union Canal which runs close by. This stocking turned out to be a great success: the fish bred and grew on well. By around 1920, thirteen years on, these fish were starting to be caught regularly by anglers. Then, suddenly, for no apparent reason, catches ceased. It was assumed that the catfish population had been wiped out by disease though no dead fish were found.

However, in 1934, almost fifteen years after the cats' mysterious disappearance, a fish of around 45lb was found dead. In 1943, nine years later, another dead fish of a similar size was found. Obviously, these were survivors of the original 1907 stocking, but still no cats of any consequence were caught with rod and line from Marsworth since the mysterious disappearance.

During this time the Woburn fish had been left well alone. Then in 1947, sixty-seven years after their stocking, the duke ordered his lakes to be netted

A big cat eventually comes to the net.

because of suspected tapeworm in the other species of fish. This netting produced several catfish, the largest weighing a staggering 70lb. The duke ordered that no catfish were to be returned or taken away from his premises, so his gamekeepers were forced to kill them.

By 1951 the duke was getting rather concerned about the disappearance of several of his rather rare ducks. So, once again, he called upon four local angling clubs to net the lakes for him. In payment for their work the clubs were offered a percentage of the fish netted out. This time two of the clubs, the Leighton Buzzard Angling Club (LBAC) and the Dawley Angling Club (DAC), asked and got permission to move some of the catfish if any were netted.

The netting yielded 48 catfish, of which the DAC had 36, and the LBAC the other 12, along with 33 fingerling zander. Two of LBAC's newly acquired catfish were stocked into the River Ouzel at Leighton Buzzard. Later one of these fish was found dead, trapped beneath a partly opened sluice gate. The other fish was never seen again.

At the time of netting LBAC had just gained the fishing rights to the middle lake in the grounds of Claydon House near Winslow. This is where they stocked their other ten fish, along with the zander. There is some dispute as to the size of the stocked Claydon fish. It is possible that the largest weighed over 40lb, although some say that the largest was only 13lb.

The DAC stocked their thirty-six fish into Withy Pool in Shropshire. Two years later seven fish had been caught, weighing between twelve and twenty pounds. The first 30lb-plus specimen to be caught on rod and line in this country came out of the middle lake at Claydon, just before Christmas in 1956. The lucky (or unlucky, as you shall see) angler was Bob Haynes. Unfortunately, this fish was foul-hooked in the dorsal fin while Bob was spinning for zander. After being taken to the local railway station in his sidecar for weighing by Jim Brennan, the bailiff, the fish was eventually returned and released. It is said that it swam off well after its ordeal. Incidentally, Jim is still the bailiff to this day, and long may he reign.

The largest of the original catfish to be caught at Claydon weighed 33lb 12oz and was caught on the first Sunday of the 1961–2 season by Reg Hutt. This later became a British Record, although it was not accepted by the British Record Fish Committee at the time of capture, despite the fact that the weighing was witnessed by over thirty people. Things don't change much.

By the 1980s there were four fish in Claydon which used to get caught,

Weed dragging is often essential.

occasionally at over thirty pounds. These fish were known at Warts, Scarface, Spot, and the brown one. The only one of these four fish that seemed to go long periods without getting caught was the largest – the brown one. How any fish can avoid capture in a water as small and as heavily fished as Claydon beats me but occasionally a fish turns up completely out of the blue. During one period the brown one managed to avoid capture for seven years.

Reg Hutt's 33lb Claydon record stood for over twenty-six years until 6.30 p.m. on Sunday 6 September 1987, when I broke it myself with a fish of 34lb 12oz. It was the brown one. It is almost certain that this is the last of the big catfish in Claydon; Warts, Spot and Scarface having probably gone.

It is now getting on for five years since any of these three has turned up at Claydon. It isn't openly known whether or not they were stolen or simply died, as they were very old fish anyway. Incidentally, the smaller known residents in Claydon have since started to pack on weight, thus showing that there is no longer the same competition for food from the bigger fish. This is probably why the brown one has grown after having a stable weight for years. It is possible that this fish is a survivor of the original stock fish from 1951.

The other stocked fish, at Marsworth Reservoir, managed to avoid capture for over fifty years. It was presumed that they had died out and become extinct in this water when suddenly, out of the blue in 1983, an angler caught a couple of kittens (small catfish) on worm while fishing for tench.

This inspired Bob Baldock and Kevin Maddocks to give Marsworth a sustained effort the following year in the hope that there must still be large parent fish inhabiting the reservoir. That year both Bob and Kevin caught fish but, unfortunately, although it was a great angling achievement, these were once again only small fish. It is unfortunate that they were not rewarded with one of the large parent fish. It's nice to think that there may still be some large fish in the reservoir, but they have avoided all attempts at capture for over fifty years. Is life really long enough to make the effort involved in fishing Marsworth worth while? I'll let you know the answer to that if ever I catch one. Fifty years without one turning up! It makes you think about burbot, doesn't it?

The history of catfish in this country isn't really complete without mention of the current record fish, which weighed 43lb 8oz. Purposely, I have left the mention of this fish until now as it is such an oddball. It was caught in 1970 by accident while the captor, Richard Bray, was pike fishing at Wilstone Reservoir, another of the Tring Complex. Wilstone is over half a mile away from Marsworth and is not connected in any way. Wilstone was never stocked legally with catfish, and to this day the 43lb fish is still the only cat ever to be caught there. This one, incidentally, was caught while the water level at Tring was lower than it had been for years as a result of a very dry summer. Obviously, this meant that a much greater area of fishable water was available to anglers. The chances of landing a bait near a large territorial catfish were greatly increased, and Mr Bray was lucky enough to drop his bait right in front of one.

The list of waters known to contain catfish is now growing rapidly. More clubs are showing an interest in stocking these fascinating, hard-fighting fish, thanks to a lot of hard work by the Catfish Conservation Group. This is not a plug as I have (perhaps wrongly) never been a member.

To conclude. Almost all the catfish in this country originate from the original fish stocked at Woburn Abbey over a hundred years ago. Up to the present time I know of four different waters that have produced catfish heavier than our present record of 43lb but none of these has been caught on rod and line.

My 34lb 12oz fish is the largest to be caught by someone fishing for them in this country, though the weight seems insignificant compared with some of the fish netted out of British waters. When you look at the weights that this species manages to attain in other countries, you will realize that our record could just about be used as bait.

In my eyes the catfish is the only species left where the record could be completely demolished rather than beaten by just a few ounces, as is the case with just about every other species in this country. Let's hope that when one is finally landed it comes to a catfish angler, for he (or she) will certainly deserve it. He will be fishing a new water and will probably be struggling, but if it's a record you want you can forget Claydon, Tiddenfoot and the rest. I don't think that the big brown one that I caught at Claydon will carry on growing to overtake the record. It is a very old fish and I just can't see it putting on a lot more weight. There are still at least two waters in this country that hold catfish in excess of our record but at the moment anglers are not allowed to fish them. Who knows what might happen in the future? I should imagine, were permission to be obtained on one of these waters, the record would be toppled pretty quickly. If one of these two waters doesn't produce the next record, then I would expect it to come again by accident from a water such as Wilstone, where catfish are no longer known to be present. I do hope that this is not the case, as it would be really terrific for a pioneering type of angler to manage to land a biggie, intentionally, from water such as Marsworth, where everyone has the chance to fish but most shy away until it has been proven that such fish exist. Good luck to anyone who is presently trying a similar place!

Catfish Basics

Shaun Harrison

RODS

Rods required for catfishing can vary enormously. The only common denominator is that the action must be of compound taper – that is, the rod must bend all the way through to the handle. Owing to the length of time that most catfish have to be fought, a fast-taper or tip-action rod simply is not suitable for the job. It is not the rod in this case that takes the strain but your arm, which means that after playing the fish heavily for a few minutes your arm ends up in too much pain to finish the job effectively. The rods that I use for almost all of my catfishing are between $1^3/_4$ and 2lb test curve and have a nice soft action. Length is a matter of personal preference. It is certainly easier to get fish into the landing net with an 11-foot rod and this is the length that most anglers tend to use. Personally, I prefer a 12-foot rod. This is for one reason only. Towards the back end of the 1986 summer I found myself having to strike at twitch bites, and I found it far easier to set the hooks with 12-foot rods. I do admit that 12-foot rods make netting the fish on your own a little more difficult, but if you do not get the hook into the catfish in the first place the netting does not even come into it at all.

Rod material is not too important, though good-quality carbon is about the nicest on which to play a fish. You tend to be able to feel better what is going on through the rod and this is obviously a big advantage in the dark. The exception to the carbon rod is when fishing for outsized catfish in very snaggy waters, where a test curve of at least $2^1/_2$lb must be used for hook-and-hold tactics. I know big carp can be held with rods with a lesser test curve and I have done it myself, but catfish simply cannot be moved easily through the water because of their shape. Carp also can only swim in one direction so each time their heads are turned you are gaining line. Turn the cat's head, though, and it will swim backwards. In these big-fish hook-and-hold situations, fibreglass is a much better rod material. Fibreglass is stronger than carbon and you are able to overload the rod more without as great a chance of the fibres parting and breaking. This can happen with even the best-quality carbons available. Perhaps fibreglass rods do not look very ultra-cult, but what does that matter if they do the job better than any carbons on the market?

REELS

Reels are a personal thing as most good-quality models will cope adequately with the job of playing a catfish. What must be remembered – and this applies to all big-fish angling – is that if your rod breaks while playing a fish you still have a chance of landing it. If, however, your reel breaks of jams you won't stand any chance whatsoever. I still use my trusty Abu Cardinal 55s. The only reason I personally have not changed my 55s is simply that I own so many spare spools and as yet they have not let me down in the eight years of constant use I have given them.

The Shimano Baitrunners are very much the reel to be seen with at the moment and they seem to perform very well. It would be interesting to see how long they will stand up to the type of pressure a big catfish can give them. The ever-faithful Mitchell 300 is a reel used by many of my friends. They might feel worn out even when you buy them but they are real cart-horses – and seem to last for ever. The three reels that I have mentioned here will all cope with English catfishing situations and all are equipped with spools large enough to hold the large quantities of the heavy line which are required when playing the fish.

LINE

Once again brand choices are a matter of personal taste. I use Sylcast for all of my catfishing as it stands up to abuse well and has good abrasion resistance. Most of my fishing, apart from the hook-and-hold situation, is done with 11lb line. Some of you may feel that that is a little strong, but wait until you hook or see a big cat on the line before you decide. I am convinced that the breaking strain of the line does not put the cats off, so why should I use a lighter one? I have never been broken by a cat yet and I intend to keep my record that way. The strength of some cats is incredible and I am sure that I would have been hard put to to have landed some of these fish on any lighter line.

HOOKLINKS

I use braided hooklinks for all of my catting. My links vary from other people's in one way. I make them long – usually about 5½ feet. This is probably why I have found no need to use lighter breaking strain main lines. My reason for the use of such long hook-links is to do with the length of the catfish's body.

Because catfish don't possess any scales I am sure that their bodies are more sensitive than most species of freshwater fish. With long, soft, braided hooklinks their bodies simply do not come into contact with the stiffer nylon. I now use Berkley 15lb braided nylon for 90 per cent of my catfishing as I have found it to withstand abrasion from the cats' teeth much better than the many other makes that I have used. Although I have not had long enough to draw up any definite conclusions on the new 25lb Silkworm marketed by Kryston, it does seem an ideal alternative to my Berkley hooklinks. My friend's father, Bill Tyson, caught a 33lb catfish in the summer of 1989 on the Kryston product along with a twenty and a large double. This is British catting at its best – especially for a seventy-year-old. None of the hooklinks was badly frayed after these battles with very large fish and this speaks highly of the Silkworm hooklength.

British catting at its best.

Another big catfish for Shaun.

HOOKS

Everyone has his own preference. I use two types. The first is a Drennan Gold Pack Super Specialist in sizes ranging from 8 to 2, depending on bait used. The second type I use is a Mustad O'Shaughnessy in similar sizes. Both these hooks are very strong and once into a catfish very rarely come out. I use singles only and never more than one at a time. Multi-hook rigs are definitely not required. Neither are the popular double hooks used for piking. Multi-hook rigs have caused the death of too many catfish to be considered in the future. Please do not add to the list of fatalities as we have not got enough big cats to spare in this country at the moment. Fortunately, the use of more than one hook at a time has now been banned on the Leighton Buzzard waters.

A lovely day and a lovely fish.

BITE DETECTION

Along with a million other anglers I use Optonics in conjunction with a monkey climber. As I walk round the banks, it would appear that my bobbins are considerably lighter in weight than those used by other anglers. This I feel is very important. I also angle my needles behind my reels as this causes less resistance to a taking catfish. The species can be very finicky and any resistance, I am sure, is the cause of most of the abortive runs that people experience. With the needles angled behind the reels, the bobbin leaves the needle and drops away from the line almost immediately rather than bouncing about up and down the needle as the line trickles off the spool. The drumming sensation that this causes passes down the line and also persuades a lot of catfish to drop the bait. The final advantage of using the bobbins behind the reel is that run clips do not have to be used to stop line falling off the spool in windy weather.

A lot of anglers seem to think that cats are in some way stupid and do not warrant this type of attention to detail. But, then again, a lot of people fail to catch many catfish. With the six barbules that catfish possess I believe that they are able to inspect terminal tackle much better than anyone realizes. For proof, consider the two most often caught catfish at Claydon – Trees and Short Feeler. Is it just coincidence that these two fish are not equipped with a proper set of barbules, or feelers – call them what you like? I personally believe not.

BAIT

Here goes! This is a piece I do not want to write but I suppose an article about catfish tackle is not really complete without a section on bait. The first thing to choose is either livebait or deadbait. Till now I have not found lives to be more effective than deads. Because of this I no longer use any kind of livebait although I do know that people swear by them. My preference is for deads as they are easier to keep and you do not have to wait for non-anglers to move away before putting your hook into a live fish. The less the general public sees of this face of angling the better, in my opinion. Of course, if you personally feel that this is the only way to catch catfish then use livebaits, but please be careful who sees you. We anglers are having enough trouble at the moment with the antis in society without making things worse for ourselves.

Under the blanket term 'deadbaits', I mean to describe boilies, mussels, liver, squid, octopus, cheese, luncheon meat, mackerel, herrings, sardines, cod fillets, eels (sand eels and freshwater eels), sausages, peanuts and, obviously numerous dead freshwater fish.

During the 1986–87 season I had a lot of success by soaking pieces of fish in various flavourings. One of my best combinations was a mixture of Catchum's Sense Appeal, blended fish oil and an emulsifier. Rather than injecting bait with flavour I found it more effective to leave baits soaking in the solution. During the early part of the 1987–88 season I started filling my baits up with flavour before actually freezing them. This method seemed to be equally effective.

The baits I am currently experimenting with are sausages. Catfish eat regular sausages anyway but, while striving for a completely different bait, I started making my own. First I obtained a selection of natural skins, though I think artificial skins would work equally well. Then I started experimenting with various weird and wonderful fillers. Using these skins has opened up a whole new field of baits that has not been considered in the past. Fortunately, these baits do not suffer from the unwanted attention of carp or bream. Both these species rip soft fish and meat baits to pieces even if they cannot fit them in their mouths whole. Another advantage with my sausage-type baits is that I can make them as heavy or as buoyant as I wish. So far, my results with these baits have been very encouraging with catfish and even with zander. I am planning to go for pike with them as well. I'm sure they will work well on some of the more heavily fished waters where a fresh approach is desperately required.

One bait that I catch a fair amount of catfish on is the mackerel head. Here is a bait that many anglers throw into the water after cutting off their preferred body sections. Pike anglers tend to do the same but if you cut a fish in half you will notice that there is far more smell in the head section than there is in the tail. This alone is a good reason for using mackerel heads. Eel sections are an excellent bait, and tend to hold artificial flavours very well indeed. This is also a tough bait, so once again it withstands the attentions of nuisance species, particularly carp and bream. Eel sections are in fact an ideal bait to use if you want to get your head down for some sleep. This, I feel, is important as one cannot fish effectively when constantly dozing and half tired. Surely a couple of hours' good sleep is better than eighteen hours of tiredness – especially if, like me, you live a long way from the venue. Remember, it is dangerous driving home when you are tired. Squid is a bait on which the catfish took a serious hammering in the beginning. Now it has become very rare to get a take on the bait. However, after leaving squid alone for a couple of seasons the cats in many places seem to be willing to take them again. All this goes to show that a lot of the original baits such as liver and water mussels are worth using again.

To conclude, I would like to say that most catfish anglers that I talk to seem to think that bait choice is not important. I have to say that I strongly disagree with this. I try to be original with my baits and for me it has certainly paid off greatly. After all, if you use and do the same things as everyone else, it stands to reason you will only catch the same – and that is not normally many catfish.

RIGS

For almost all of my catfishing I freeline. When I use a lead I tend to use one of at least $1^1/_2$oz and never with a backstop. I use this rather large lead to try to create as little resistance as possible. I had better explain. If a fish takes a bait and swims sideways a small lead drags and causes resistance. If, however, a $1^1/_2$oz lead is substituted, this tends to grip in silt and allows free passage of the line through a semi-buoyant ledger bead.

I do not use backstops and bolt-rig-style methods as I do not have confidence in them. I know catfish do get caught by anglers using these rigs but I am sure that they miss out on many chances. The main reason, I think, is to do with the mouth of the catfish. Again, I had better explain. Fixed-lead rigs are an excellent way to catch carp and tench but a catfish's mouth is far bigger and wider than that of a carp. This means that the hook is less likely to catch hold on the way out of the catfish's mouth. Also, there is a lot more bone inside the cat's mouth, which makes a hookhold much harder to find than in the case of a carp.

Dylan Wrathal and his friends catch a lot of carp and a lot of cats on fixed leads with livebaits. Dylan told me that during one close season he was lucky enough to see cats chasing live fish but they did not appear to be very successful in catching them. The only way the cats could catch smaller fish was to sit and ambush them. So the reasoning is that a catfish is more likely to take a fish with a weight anchoring it down and therefore unable to swim off.

I am very keen on hitting twitches when I am catfishing. My twitcher hitting for catfish began by accident. I was being pestered by what I thought were carp or bream taking my baits. Like everyone else I was sitting there infuriated as the bobbins were going up an inch and stopping. I decided that the only way to scare these nuisance fish off would be to try and hook a few and let them swim around the shoal. I reasoned that a panicking hooked fish would scatter the rest of its companions and give the catfish a better chance of finding my bait. I wound in a rod, put on a smaller bait and recast. After a short while the bobbin twitched again and I pulled back a couple of feet. I sat with my hand hovering over the reel ready to strike. A couple of minutes later I saw the line trembling in the rings on the same rod. This time I struck immediately before the bobbin moved, and the rod wrenched round. It turned out to be a 21lb 5oz catfish. In the following few weeks I had a steady run of big catfish after receiving only the tiniest indications. During this period I was also just about the only angler still putting catfish on the bank. I saw others having chances but all were ignored. All were dismissed as bream bites. Some of my catfish at this time did not even move the bobbin and I just noticed the line flicker at the rod tip or quiver in the rings. This was tiring fishing but well worth it.

AFTER A RUN

Now that I have described what gear and bait to use I had better go through what happens when you actually get a run. In the early season you should get a steady take similar to a pike run on a deadbait. Simply pick up the rod, shut the bail arm and strike hard. Remember that the hook point may be resting against bone so it will take considerable force to set it. Do not wind down to feel for the fish as many people do when piking, as this generally causes the cat to drop the bait. With luck you will have hooked your fish. If not, recast in the same area immediately; occasionally the fish will give you a second chance.

If you have connected, hold the fish hard for a couple of seconds to make sure the hook is in well. I think that cats are like pike in so far as you hook them when they try to eject the bait. The resulting fight can vary immensely. Some fight fast; some fight very slowly but powerfully. The latter type of fight generally indicates a big fish. Catfish normally need to be played hard to keep them on the move. If you start to play them lightly they will swim about the lake all afternoon as though they are not even hooked. The fun starts when the cat reaches the landing net. Forget all you have ever read or learned about netting fish. There is no way you can wait until its tail is over the drawcord before lifting the net. If you do this the cat's head will probably be touching the hand of the netsman half-way up the handle. Instead, pull the fish until its head reaches the spreader block, then scoop the rest of it in. The bigger fish tend to wrap their tails round the drawcord so they have to be shaken in quite firmly. Obviously the drawcord must be very stout. It is essential to have a landing net with arms of at least 42 inches to stand a chance of netting a big fish and a 50 inch net is far better. My biggest catfish at the time of writing weighed just under 35lb and needed to be shaken five times before it folded into the net – and this was by a very experienced angler who had netted many big cats for other men.

ON THE BANK

Once a cat is safely in the net, lift it carefully on to some wet grass or a wet sack. Look after catfish on the bank – we do not have many in this country. One dead cat is the equivalent of hundreds of dead carp and pike. The cat's mouth is very tough so I find it easiest to unhook them with a Drennan specimen tube-end disgorger.

Once a fish has been unhooked it will probably need weighing and this is when most newcomers realize that the weigh sling they have used for numerous 20lb carp simply is not big enough to weigh a catfish. Kevin Nash's big sling is only just big enough to weigh a scraper of twenty and I use his monster piker sling, which is almost purpose-built for catfish. This cradles a twenty-pounder with ease. Holding a decent cat for a photo tends to cause problems for most people. The easiest way I have found is to trap the farside

The decent way to hold a big catfish.

pectoral fin between the fingers and hold the other hand just down past the vent. This tends to make the tail droop but unless you get someone else to help you display it you cannot do much about that.

One final point. Please do not retain cats for any period of time. I say this because in a conventional carp sack they tend to get the soft nylon material stuck in their teeth. This then tightens material round their gills, preventing them from breathing properly. This has led to the death of at least one very big catfish, so do not let us lose a second in this way. The new tube-type retainers such as the Kevin Nash Cat Tunnel or the ET Cat Tube are far better retaining systems. In my opinion the Nash Tunnel is a better choice because of the zip-open top which makes the removal of the fish far easier and safer.

Rudd in Danger

Alan Rawden, in the chapter that follows, stresses the present-day fragility of rudd populations and I can only sadly agree. In 1986, Roger Miller and I discovered the most paradisiacal of rudd lakes, totally isolated in the Wensum valley. If a lake could have everything, Forbidden did: shallows, deeper holes, vast weeping willows, luxuriant beds of white water-lilies and the healthiest stock of rudd between 8oz and 2lb imaginable. Every single fish was a fragment of nature's perfection and nobody knew. We would break no records there but we went over and over again simply to catch these beautiful fish.

In 1989 I visited the lake early in the season – only for an hour or two, just long enough to catch a handful of beauty. Forbidden had, in a few months,

The secluded world of the summer stillwater. Forbidden at its peak.

become ugly. The willow had fallen in. The water had drained away and on the bare mudflats the lilies rotted. Of rudd there was no sign at all. Boreholes, it emerged, sunk around the valley to supply new estates, had lowered the water table still further and Forbidden and its precious stock of rudd were lost for ever.

Such has been the case in pools all around the country and a once-prolific species can now be found only in localized pockets. Since the 1960s more and more waters have been stocked with carp and this comparatively large, fast-growing and voracious species has had a very detrimental effect on the more delicate rudd everywhere. Since the 1960s also, agricultural pollution has gradually eradicated rudd populations as well as a great many estate lakes which were once the seemingly enviable citadels of the species. Pike anglers, too, have done their bit to destroy the rudd fishing that our grandfathers knew. Removing rudd for livebaits has, in places, ended populations. Perhaps worse has been the introduction of roach livebaits into previously strictly rudd and pike waters. Roach survivors and escapees have interbred with the rudd and after a few generations the water has been left with a stock of hybrids – fine fish in themselves but not the true rudd sought by the specialist or naturalist

Forbidden today.

angler. Tragically, the great rudd waters of western Ireland have been hit in this way and the roach is appearing more and more in the traditional rudd loughs. County Clare still has rudd stocks but the man who wants to sample true Irish rudd fishing – which means the best in the world – must hurry to get his plans under way.

For the more adventurous, there are rudd populations abroad. Certainly the most dramatic that I can attest to lives in lake Bled in northern Yugoslavia. This is a truly fairy-tale lake of magical beauty – in the evening especially, when the castle is silhouetted by the setting sun, the restaurants glow and the bands play alongside the promenade. The only rudd I saw were immaculate fish of absolutely authentic gold and red up to a pound or so in weight. However, I was assured that much larger fish live out in the lake, only coming in close as light fails. Regrettably, during my visit, I was more interested in the catfish and I feel that I let a really good opportunity slip by.

Of course, rudd are not alone in facing problems in the modern world. Eel populations are under severe threat from commercial netsmen. Wild carp are being lost in old silting ponds, which are being filled in more and more for agricultural, industrial or home development. Crucian carp, because they are a difficult, secretive fish, are almost always overlooked in any stocking policy.

The classic shape of the fully scaled carp.

What a tragedy if wildies were ever to disappear.

It does seem that some of our oldest, most traditional species are under severe threat and it was good to talk very recently to Broadsman John Nunn.

John has just been offered the management of a private, enclosed broad of some half a dozen acres and his plan is to try to provide a sanctuary for all the above-mentioned threatened species. Fishing there will be of an unusual sort, the type our grandfathers used to enjoy. The water will, I hope, be large enough to accommodate fish which are about to lose their own homes. Had I known this a year ago, for example, the better rudd at Forbidden could have been saved, perhaps. How good it is to see someone do something for the less glamorous smaller species! I am sure he will have every assistance possible from all anglers of discernment.

Fishing for Rudd

Alan Rawden

I think it is fair to say that rudd are not the most popular fish and that sadly rudd fishing does not command the kudos that is attributed to modern-day carp and pike fishing. The circumstances surrounding this apparent lack of popularity are somewhat complex, but the main reason is the scarcity of the fish. There are not many rudd around, especially good ones. I would be surprised if there were more than a handful of decent rudd waters in this country.

Looking at England in the early 1990s, the future for the rudd angler looks decidedly bleak. I feel that owing to a general lack of imagination among water authorities, angling clubs, and fishery owners in general, rudd fishing could become at best a novelty and at worst a thing of the past. Rudd are perhaps

Alan admires a very big fish.

Alan admires two more monsters.

a forgotten fish, a fish of the past, and I honestly feel that unless serious measures are undertaken to reintroduce these beautiful but maligned fish to more waters they could, with the passing of time, die out completely. If there is such an animal as a rudd angler, it is usually the one who is rather fortunate in finding a rudd water near his home. I would strongly advise such an angler to make the most of his luck as the life span of most rudd waters is usually quite short.

As with tench and bream, and most other species, the respective waters will peak and decline over a period of years. However, with rudd these peaks and declines appear to be much more prominent. Once a water begins to peak, which is very often a result of one or two year classes coming to the fore, the water will possibly suffer a rapid increase in angling pressure, the rudd will then suffer and the water will fall into decline. This situation happens on all waters, with all fish, but rudd and their waters appear to be much more sensitive to pressure and the decline is more rapid. Where big rudd are concerned, it is highly likely that the numbers of fish present are low. The usual situation is that a few survivors from a particular year class have waxed fat on a very rich water and have also for one reason or another avoided the attentions of the big-fish fraternity.

From this preamble the reader will quite rightly deduce that rudd fishing is in a very fragile state and that the fish are desperately in need of the respect they deserve. Rudd are fish of the summer and they immediately conjure up visions of tranquil evenings and balmy summer nights on lush, secluded pools. Much of my rudd fishing has been exactly that and, to be honest, when I haven't caught fish it didn't really matter.

DISTRIBUTION

The distribution of rudd throughout the British Isles is somewhat patchy, to say the least. The discovery of knowledge of a rudd water is rather a result of good fortune than anything else. Realistically, anyone contemplating fishing for rudd would be well advised to consider fishing in Ireland, for rudd and rudd waters are comparatively common in certain areas of the Emerald Isle. Almost all the lakes along the Shannon catchment area contain rudd, and in many cases the fish are numerous and grow to a good size. Historically, rudd in Britain were much more numerous, and waters were distinctly more widespread. However, it has to be said that rudd and the waters that hold them have never enjoyed such widespread distribution as tench or bream.

An old shot of Irish rudding.

Probably one of the few actual strongholds for rudd was the Norfolk Broads and the surrounding fens of East Anglia. Here the rudd thrived in the wild, rushy and often neglected habitat. Elsewhere in the country rudd waters seemed to crop up 'here and there'. These waters were as diverse as the areas in which they were situated. A notable example of such a water is Ringmere near Wretham in Norfolk, where the Revd E.C. Alston caught his record fish of 4lb 8oz in 1933. Alston also caught a number of other large rudd during a period of several years in the 1930s. Another water which produced a number of big rudd in the past was Slapton Ley in Devon. During a period between 1930 and 1950 the water produced fish in excess of 4lb for a number of anglers fortunate enough to fish there. A number of other notable waters have also appeared over the years from areas as diverse as the Lake District, the Midlands and the Home Counties.

Today the distribution of rudd waters is somewhat limited. The Norfolk Broads and surrounding fens still hold a somewhat diminished population of fish but generally the fish are not widespread and are of no great size. As in the past, the occasional water seems to crop up; rural Norfolk, the east Midlands and a few other counties of England can rightfully boast the possession of waters which have produced big rudd during the 1980s.

RUDD WATERS AND LOCATION

Rudd appear to thrive in large waters. This point is classically illustrated when we look at the Lakes of Southern Ireland, the Norfolk Broads, and certain east Midlands reservoirs that have produced fish over the years. However, not all waters that produce rudd are particularly large. Anything from estate lakes to farm ponds might hold fish in varying degrees of size and quantity.

Generally speaking, I feel that anyone wishing to fish for rudd should choose a water actually known to hold them, as any attempt to try to find a rudd water on a trial-and-error basis would be extremely chancy. The local or national grapevine is probably the best way to find such a water. The angling press and tackle shops may help with location, but as rudd waters are rather thin on the ground information is somewhat exclusive. Having found or chosen his rudd water, the angler should then set about trying to locate fish within the water itself. Location of rudd depends mainly on the size of the water and the numbers of fish present.

Rudd are a highly mobile fish, which partially explains why they appear to thrive in larger waters. The degree of mobility is really dependent on factors such as the numbers of fish present, plant life and weed growth, the depth of

Rudd and tench so often live together in a well-balanced environment.

the water, the weather, and many others. No two rudd waters are the same, but several identifiable characteristics common on most waters can aid in the location of fish. Rudd like cover, whether the cover is in the form of floating weedbeds such as bistort, potamogeton or water-lilies, subsurface weed, or beds of rushes.

Many of these weedier areas of the water will naturally coincide with shallower areas, and in clear water the rudd can often be seen moving in and around these weedbeds, or from one weedbed to another.

While rudd can be fished for and caught in deeper water, it is generally recognized that they are predominantly mid-water-to-surface feeders. Bearing this in mind, it is quite understandable why rudd will spend much of their time in the shallower and weedier areas: it is simply because the snails and larvae which form a large part of their staple diet are to be found there.

Where rudd cannot be visually observed in and around the weedy shallows, they will often give away their presence by rolling at feeding periods. These are often in the late evening or early morning, and sometimes throughout the night. This rolling can sometimes take the form of a periodic roll of an individual fish, or often a shoal can be observed rolling at frequent intervals. It is often possible to track the movement of a shoal, as they can often be seen to be rolling along the surface on a particular route. By using a degree of anticipation, the angler will find it possible to ambush the shoal at a suitable point. Prior to fishing, the angler would be well advised to visit the water during the recognized feeding periods and watch for rolling fish. If the fish are to be seen rolling regularly in certain areas, a hot spot will have been found, and should be likely to produce fish when fishing commences.

It is essential that the angler does not confuse the rolls of rudd with rolling tench and bream. While it is not always possible to define the rolls of any fish easily, the respective rolls of both tench and bream are not that dissimilar but are usually totally different from the rolls of rudd. Tench and bream rolls could be roughly described as being a smooth glide. However, the roll of a rudd is a much more noisy affair and could be best described as a slash or even a smack.

The number of rudd present in a water is usually mirrored by the numbers of fish seen rolling. In waters where only a few large specimens are present, watching for rolling fish can be a rather tedious exercise. Often few, if any, fish can be seen rolling and in these circumstances a degree of intuition on the part of the angler is required.

A roach by fin placement, but a rudd around the mouth perhaps.

Two giant rudd dwarf the Mitchell reel.

With regard to actually fishing for rudd, two distinct styles emerge. On one hand we have a style where the angler is fishing shallow water, or the shallower part of the deeper water, where rudd can often be located visually and can be caught on or near the surface. This style of fishing may often involve stalking fish from either the bank or from a boat in daylight.

The other style of fishing is fishing open, deeper water. Here location will be much more difficult, and with rolling fish to go by only at feeding periods the angler will be fishing blind for much of the time.

TACKLE

Tackle for rudd fishing may not need to be terribly sophisticated. Most specialist anglers will possess the required rods, reels and sundries necessary to catch rudd. A selection of hooks from 6–16 and lines from 3–5lb BS, a range of floats for fishing both day and night, and a reasonable selection of larger weights and swimfeeders will also be required.

Probably the only aspect of tackle which requires any degree of specialization is the rods. While most rods will catch rudd, the use of a rod that is too stiff

Night fishing for rudd can be very productive.

or powerful will often result in the loss of fish. Owing to the manner in which rudd respond when hooked, it is necessary to use a softer through-actioned rod. When big rudd are hooked and pressure is applied to move fish away from weeds or snags, the fish often come to the surface and tend to do a lot of splashing about. This is also noticeable when the fish are brought to the net. The use of a rod which is too stiff will often pull the hook out in these situations.

The rods I use for most of my rudd fishing are 12-foot carbons of 1 $^1/_4$lb test curve. Whilst these rods are not suited for very long distances, they are excellent light-to-medium ledger and feeder rods and they also make an ideal float rod.

BAITS AND METHODS

As with tackle, the baits necessary for rudd fishing are fairly elementary. Maggots, worms and sweetcorn are all excellent baits, but for sheer consistency the best bait by far is without doubt bread, fished either as crust or flake. Perhaps the reason why bread is such a successful bait is that it can fished in so many different ways. Possibly its main advantage over other baits is that it has a degree of buoyancy. It can be fished on the surface or at mid-water or on the bottom by a wise variety of uncomplicated methods.

When the angler has located some rudd in shallower water and at relatively close range, it may be found that the fish will take baits either on the surface, at mid-water or on the bottom. Quite often in these situations the fish will take a bait as long as it is in the swim. Where fish are located in shallower water and at relatively close range, freeline fishing with either crust or flake is as good as anything. Corn can also be used with some success in these situations, though it may be necessary to pinch a swanshot on to the line to add a little weight as an aid to casting.

Another useful bait to use in this situation is an air-injected lobworm. This bait can either be fished freeline on the surface or anchored to the bottom with a swanshot. Although freelining is both a successful and an uncomplicated method, its use is somewhat limited, especially where lengthy casts are necessary and in windy conditions. In these situations an alternative method has to be employed.

A rudd of classic form.

The most suitable alternatives to freelining are either float fishing or fishing with a floating ledger. Although the two methods are basically similar, there are a number of subtle differences in their use. Float fishing is essentially a tool to aid bite indication and is best employed when using particle baits such as maggots or corn at fairly short range, especially when rather finicky bites are expected. The size and weight of the float is really dictated by such factors as the distance at which it is necessary to fish, the strength of the wind and sub-surface drag. For daylight float fishing I usually opt for simple peacock quill with the line attached to the bottom end only. A two- or three-swanshot float suffices for most situations and there is a rarely any need for elaborate shotting patterns. I usually bulk most of the shot around the float and perhaps have a BB shot about 6 inches from the hook to sink the line.

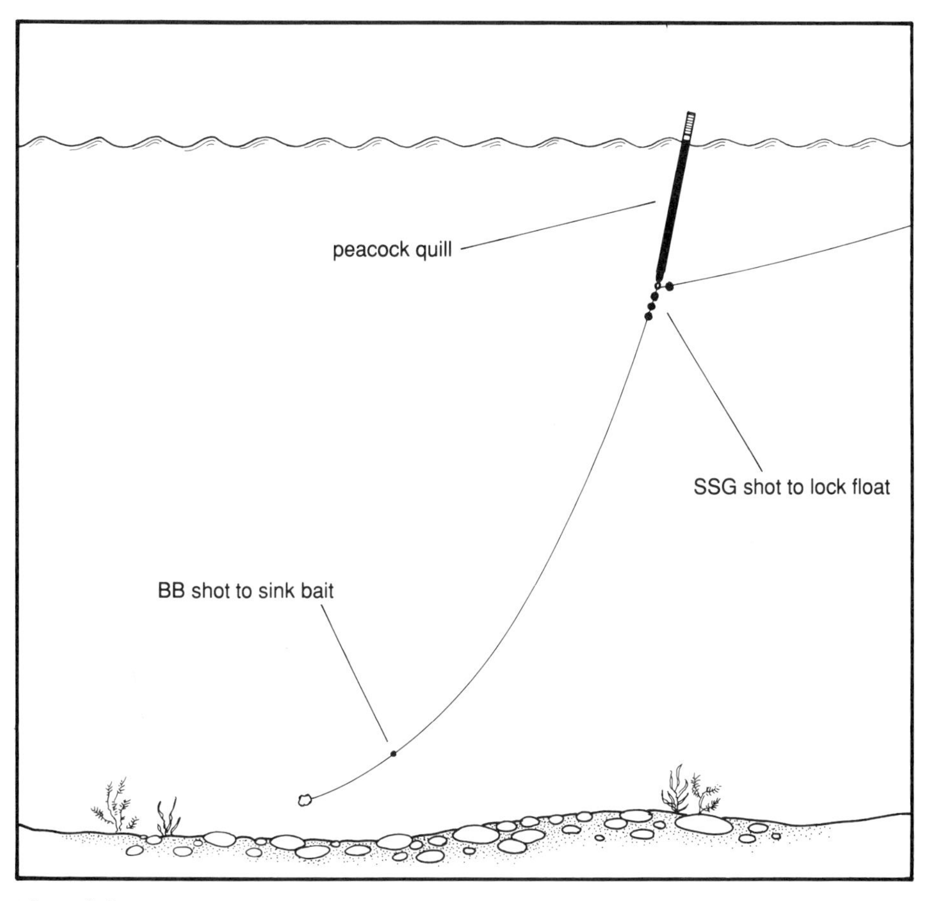

Float-fishing rig.

If or when it becomes necessary to float fish after dark, I simply change the peacock quill for a Betalight float. When fishing after dark it is essential to have an intimate knowledge of any weedbeds in the surrounding area or floats may become snagged and possibly lost. I would strongly advise the use of a weaker hooklink when fishing after dark. In the event of the float snagging the hooklink should theoretically break first, enabling the angler to retrieve the expensive Betalight without much trouble.

I remember fishing for rudd on a Shropshire lake several years ago. I was float fishing a very weedy swim, and on at least half a dozen occasions I became snagged and broke my line. On each occasion I nearly lost an expensive Betalight float. Had I not set up a spinning rod to retrieve my tackle I would have surely lost a number of floats for good. On that occasion I was using 4lb BS line straight through to the hook, but on my next visit to the water I used a 3lb hooklink with 4lb main line. Although I did lose the occasional hook there were comparatively few problems.

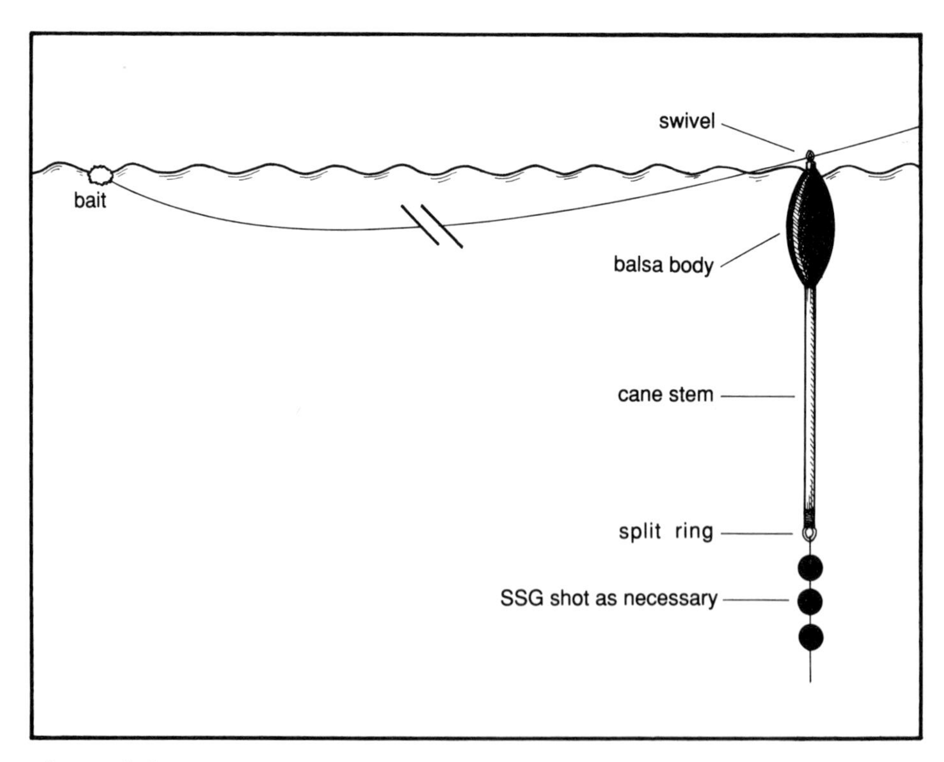

Floating ledger.

Chris Turnbull clutches two huge rudd of over 3lb.

Situations will crop up in which the float becomes ineffective and something of a problem to use; occasions will occur when windy weather severely restricts the use of a float, or when the angler finds it necessary to fish at a range where float fishing ceases to be a practicable method. On these occasions I tend to favour the use of a floating ledger, which is basically a cross between float fishing and freelining. The beauty of using a floating ledger is that it enables the angler to retain the advantages of freelining while still being able to suspend a bait from the surface and having a much greater casting range at the same time.

When I originally started using floating ledgers, I used one of my own design which was initially developed from a stick ledger used for tench fishing. In recent years, however, some excellent 'controllers' designed for floater fishing for carp have appeared on the market. These can be effectively used as floating ledgers, but they do have limitations. First, the weight of the controller cannot be adjusted and, second, being usually somewhat bulky in design, they do not cast as well as a purpose-built floating ledger.

My design of floating ledger is basically a balsa barrel with a swivel at the top and a cane stem below. At the bottom end of the cane stem a split ring is attached (which was originally used for holding an Arlesey bomb). A short length of thickish line is attached to the split-ring, to which a desired number of swanshot are attached. More can be added or taken away as required. Bite indication with the floating ledger is usually achieved by watching the line, or the bait, or both. These floating ledgers can be cast a considerable way, which is quite an advantage when rudd are spotted rolling at a distance which would be inaccessible with normal float tackle.

The floating ledger is set up in a similar manner to an ordinary submerged ledger. The ledger is stopped at a desired distance away from the hook bait by a swivel, a Drennan ring, or a plastic ledger stop. The length of tail is decided by the type of bait being used and what sort of presentation is required.

I remember fishing Lough Annaghmore in southern Ireland in the early eighties. I was fishing from a boat and the rudd could be found on the shallow reedy bars which are quite prevalent on the water. Initially the fish were caught by being spotted at close quarters and being tempted by freelined flake. However, after several days of fairly intense fishing the rudd became very wary of the boats and their occupants. Fortunately, by this time a number of regular holding areas had been located, and to avoid continuously frightening the fish I anchored the boat a safe distance away from the hot spots and cast a floating leger to the rudd without frightening them. Needless to say, the method was highly successful.

When fishing for rudd in shallow and often clear water, the use of groundbait is not really necessary, and in many cases groundbaiting can do positively more harm than good. Daylight fishing in these sort of circumstances is basically a matter of stalking fish and then casting to them. The whole operation is rather instant and the angler will not have time for groundbait.

ALTERNATIVES TO FLOAT FISHING

Most of the rudd waters to be found in England will often be devoid of any great areas of weedy shallow water and consequently the general character of the water may take the form of a somewhat featureless lake, gravel pit, or reservoir. In this situation a much more static approach is required. Although it may still be possible to catch rudd on or near the surface, the emphasis will shift to bottom- or mid-water-feeding fish. This approach to rudd fishing will be basically similar to fishing for tench or bream, and will often involve the use of one or more rods, bite alarms and all that is generally required to achieve success in this style of fishing. The methods of fish location are similar to those employed when fishing shallower, weedier water. Although it will probably not be possible to stalk fish, the angler will have to locate fish by watching for surface activity at recognized feeding periods. If the water appears to be devoid of any surface activity it is advisable to keep on the move until fish are located. I have very often found that if rudd are in an area being fished they will usually be caught. Once fish are located in this manner it pays to continue fishing the area until blanks start to occur. Once this happens it is time to move swims and find fish elsewhere.

Roger Miller with two big rudd.

The jutting lower lip of the rudd.

The methods that can be employed on these larger, more featureless waters are numerous and varied. Float fishing can be an excellent method both day and night and probably the only method to catch fish successfully in the margins. Unfortunately, float fishing does have a number of failings. First, it is not a suitable method for fishing anywhere other than the margins or at fairly close range. On certain waters it may be necessary to fish at distances of sixty or seventy yards or more and float fishing at this range is a distinctly unrealistic proposition. Another problem with float fishing is that its effectiveness is considerably influences by weather conditions: it becomes an extremely tedious method in windy weather, especially where a reasonable cast is necessary.

Alongside a number of technical problems I also find over a fairly long session float fishing can be a somewhat wearisome experience, especially on hard water. Float fishing is a most enjoyable method when there is a reasonable amount of action. However, when the fishing is rather slow, float fishing is not a method I particularly enjoy.

The alternatives to float fishing are either ledgering or swimfeeder fishing. Ledgering is the method most suited to fishing at extreme ranges of seventy yards or more. However, I personally find that whacking out bait attached to a ledger rig for rudd is of somewhat limited appeal.

For general rudd fishing I feel much happier using a swimfeeder as it enables me to present a bait with a small amount of loose feed in the same area. If groundbait is used to prebait a certain area and the cast is not always as accurate as to be spot on the baited area, the presence of a small amount of loose feed from the feeder will to a certain degree compensate for any shortcomings. I tend to favour open-end feeders for rudd fishing as they allow me to use a wide range of loose feed. The usual format is to use maggots inside the feeder and plug each end with crumb groundbait. Although the maggots serve as loose feed, the crumb groundbait is equally important as it acts as an attractor. In both ledgering and swimfeeder fishing for rudd I prefer to use a long tail. With buoyant or semi-buoyant baits a much better presentation can be achieved with the running link.

Night fishing for rudd in the Felbrigg heyday.

The rig I use is simplicity itself. The feeder is stopped by a small swivel and a bead to prevent the knot clogging the eye of the feeder link. The length of the tail and the size of the hook obviously vary with the type of bait being used. With flake I use either a size 8 or 10 hook and a tail of at least 3 feet. With maggots, worms or corn I would use a link of about 2 feet with the hook size corresponding to the size of the bait. The main reason for using a long tail for bread is that it takes the weight of the feeder further away from the bait and thus allows it to sink much more slowly and possibly to remain buoyant. Any feeding fish in the area will spot the bait earlier and, with luck, take it more freely.

Rudd are by nature very inquisitive fish and will often be attracted by the splash of a feeder entering the water, especially when they are in a feeding mood. Bites can be expected very soon after casting out and a bait that is still buoyant will be seen much more easily and taken much more quickly than a bait that has sunk rapidly to the bottom. To avoid a bread bait that is nailed to the bottom it is necessary to use the right sort of bread. The best bread to use if buoyancy is required is the old-fashioned crusty farmhouse type of loaf. What to look for is a light, fluffy crumb. Avoid the rather gooey, stodgy type of bread we associate with the sliced wrapped loaves more commonly used.

The perfect rudd . . . held by Alan Rawden.

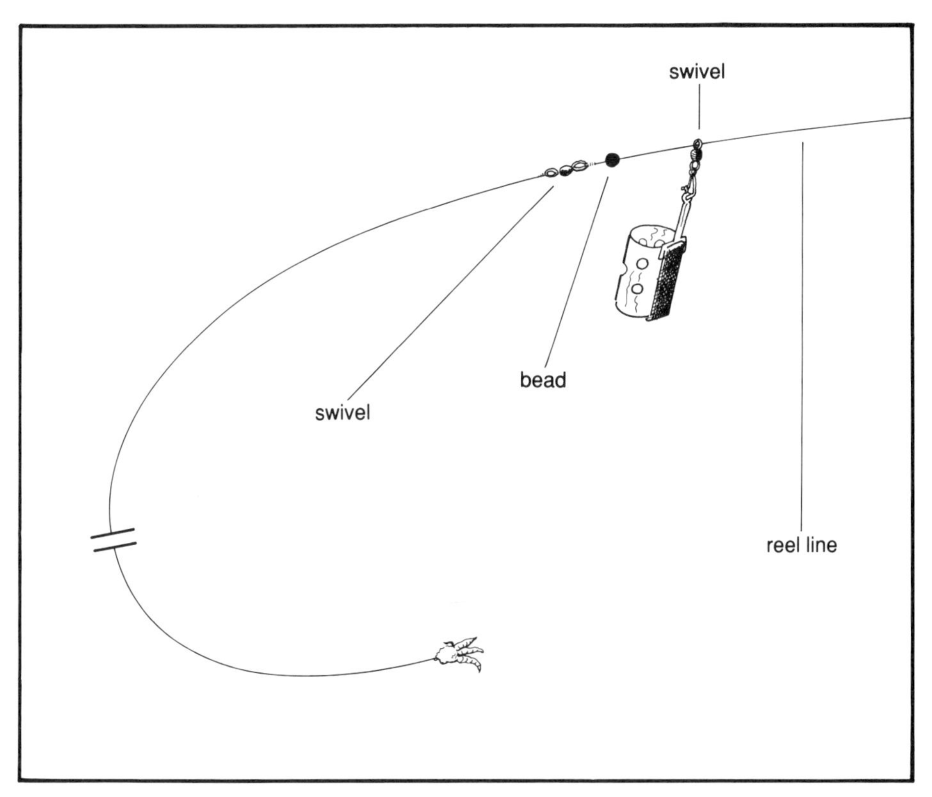

The feeder rig.

The other commonly used baits, such as maggots, corn and worms, will all catch fish, but more buoyant baits are often more successful. A number of my rudd-fishing friends have caught a lot of big fish by adding a piece of flake to the maggots on the hook. This gives the bait a degree of buoyancy and makes it more attractive to the fish. Worms can also be made to float by injecting them with air from a hypodermic syringe and corn can also be made to float by adding a small piece of polystyrene to the bait. Whilst rudd can often be caught quite easily on bottom baits, the addition of a little buoyancy will usually give the angler the edge.

In ledgering and feeder-fishing it is often necessary to use groundbait. Because rudd are a highly mobile fish groundbait has a twofold purpose: first, it acts as an attractor to any passing fish and, second, it acts as a food source to hold any fish that might stop. The type of groundbait required for rudd fishing is fairly standard, and consists of a 50/50 mixture of white and brown breadcrumb. To this I will add a quantity of maggots, and sometimes hemp

The boat, the duck and the rudd.

and corn. I have tried using a mashed bread groundbait, in which the loose particles of bread float to the surface to attract any nearby rudd. However, as this ploy usually attracts most of the waterfowl on the water I am often rather reluctant to use it.

In conclusion, rudd fishing can be as hard or as easy as the angler wants to make it. In this age of increasingly stereotyped fishing, new challenges are somewhat hard to come by. Rudd fishing is not as easy as it may outwardly appear and can offer a very pleasant challenge indeed.

Rudd from a Boat

Alan Rawden is probably the most successful big-rudd angler at the present time and there is little to add to this expert advice. However, on the isolated Irish loughs, the Broads – where, thank God, rudd are recovering in places – and on many large stillwaters, a boat is most vital for approaching this species.

It is impossible to overstate how shy rudd shoals can be, in clear water especially. For the majority of their time they will hang along unapproachably overgrown banks, in distant reedbeds, in isolated bays, deep in reedbeds or far out in open water. In these circumstances the only way to get a bait to them at all is by boat.

Forbidden Lake produces yet again.

Roger Miller with lovely rudd.

The boat needs to be stable and must be propelled by the most stealthy rowing or careful poling. Most of my time out is simply spent drifting with the wind, making as little vibration as is humanly possible. Low-slung stools are ideal to fish from and cushioning of some sort on the floor and the sides of the boat is invaluable. Binoculars are indipensable to see the shoals priming one or even two hundred yards off and to make the most unobtrusive approach possible.

I always try to stop some thirty to fifty yards from the shoal; any closer, in my experience, and they are likely to spook. I use 3 or 4lb line, well smeared in ET line grease, either a bubble float or a carp controller, soft, semi-buoyant flake on a size 8 hook or a floating Chum Mixer biscuit on a size 10 hook. Takes to the flake are generally instant but sometimes a score or more of floaters are needed before the rudd come to the surface to bite confidently.

All smiles despite the drizzle.

On the strike and immediately afterwards, I try to draw the fish as far away from the rest of the shoal as quickly as possible. Being as swift as possible, I have rarely found it possible to boat more than four or five fish, especially larger ones, before the rest become unsettled and swim purposefully away.

Above all, boat rudd fishing is fun. There is a lovely element of doing things the traditional, Crabtree way and of following in the footsteps of the Broadland maestro, Dennis Pye. The freedom of the water, the beauty of the wild, untrodden reedbanks, the blue skies filled with unexpected bird life, all put summer rudd fishing in a class of its own. I do believe that once tried it is hard to go back to the limitations of traditional bank fishing.

Possibly the very best time to be afloat is the twilight period after a long, still, hot summer's day – just when the swallows are at their most active and the first bats are beginning to flit. This is exactly when some of the larger rudd appear, those very big, very cautious fish that have been hiding deep in reed- or weedbeds throughout the day. As Alan Rawden describes, this is when they roll with a vengeance – often after the moths fluttering like snowflakes on the mirror of the pool. I dare say it is possible to catch a really huge fish on the dry fly. I have never done it. Not yet. But that is the beauty of angling – its treasures are never utterly exhausted.

Spooked Fish

I first began to pursue big rudd seriously in the early part of the 1970s on Norfolk lakes which at that time were virtually pristine. I frequently found that fish were so ridiculously easy that soon I had a quite inflated opinion of my rudding ability. This situation did not last for long as rudd populations on water after water quickly cottoned on to my activities. I kept a rudd diary for a while, a part of which I published in *The Big Fish Scene* edited in 1978 by Frank Guttfield. I chose two typical entries which showed that the first three sessions would be very productive and thereafter catches would taper off dramatically. I was fortunate then in fishing private or unknown waters quite rich in rudd: transpose the situation to a hard fish water and it is easy to see why big rudd are rare creatures, spooked very easily by baits and lines.

The great days of Felbrigg Lake.

An early Felbrigg rudd success.

There are, of course, ways to combat this, just as there are with any fish. Long-distance casting can be an answer at times if the water is relatively weed-free. This worked for me on Norfolk's Warren Lake when I could not get any fish closer in and when I found an attractive gravel bar seventy or eighty yards farther out. That lake was weedy and preparing the swim took a great deal of time, I remember, but the rewards were worth it over five or six sessions.

The second approach is to look for the more unusual, neglected swims. I have spent a good deal of rudding time wading about in reedbeds and the shallower snaggy, weeded areas, searching for tiny clear swims where a bait can be presented. Occasional very large rudd hang up during the day in the most overgrown of areas that you find in older pits and lakes.

New baits have often given sport a brief boost. Maggots flavoured with pineapple and maple, I remember, gave sport a fillip at that most famous of Norfolk lakes, Felbrigg. Air-injected worms picked up the odd fish, and now I have no doubt that various mini-boilies would work well for fish over $1^1/_2$lb.

After a while, the rudd approached any bait with a great deal of caution and I found it necessary to scale down both hook size and line strength. At these times I began to use a fixed paternoster rather than a running link and

A rudd drawn from the sanctuary of the weeping willow.

Forbidden could provide hectic sport – if it was rested frequently.

the tail length often had to be 4 or 5 feet. Bites became far less bold and the days of the indicator ramming itself into the butt ring were history. By now it was a case of sitting on the rods and hitting the smallest lifts and tremors. One fine rudd grassed by Andrew Hitchings, I remember, simply wrinkled the line as it entered the water. That event made quite an impression on me and I embarked on serious twitcher hitting. It was a tiring game but often worked: a single twitch at 1 a.m. could result in a fabulous fish.

Good rudd waters are virtually all crystal-clear but if you can hit them when they are clouded fireworks can result. On just three occasions in my life I have been on rudd waters after serious storms have completely coloured them. Each time the rudd have been all but suicidal and on one occasion I landed as many rudd in five hours as I had done in the previous six weeks. A more reliable approach is to fish the waters at the back end of the season, especially if the last months go out wild, wet and windy. Such exceptional bags can result in February and March that they can make you wonder if summer fishing for rudd is worth while at all. Probably, though, if more people fished at this stage of the year the rudd would behave with their usual frustrating aloofness.

Should you be fortunate enough to find rudd in a private, secret water then fish sparingly, resting the shoals for long periods. This is an obvious way to combat the big rudd's habitual wariness. Probably this is the only fair way to approach such a rare and sensitive species. Certainly, in the great days of Forbidden, Miller and I fished a maximum of three times a season and we know we could have fish each time. We felt we were doing little harm to the place and having our fun when we wished. Nature has her own ways of telling you to go easy and to obey her does nothing but good.

EELS

It is not hard to understand the appeal of the eel for so many people. Even in looks a big eel is impressive. I will not say that it is beautiful for beauty is very much in the eye of the beholder, but its sinewy, powerful form cannot be ignored or scorned. Personally, I have found the eyes of the eel compelling ever since I first focused on them thirty-odd years ago. The way they swim, too, is mesmerizing, magical – a disappearing act of nature. As recently as May 1990 I was watching the water under a fish cage in a Scottish loch. The sun burned down and every pebble, every trout's spot was visible. So was a great,

A perfect eel pond.

black, serpentine form on the gravel bed, which, as if feeling my gaze, wound itself into rapid action and disappeared in seconds under the shadow of the cage. I spent minutes waiting for it to reappear. It did not. I left with the knowledge that I had seen the great eel and yet with the feeling that it was all illusion.

Illusion, myth and mystery have, since earliest times, surrounded the eel. The Greeks adored eels, believed that they were goddesses in disguise and paid vast sums of money for the luxury of eating them. Eels have also been regarded as a stimulant for the voice and the smoke of burning eel was said to ease childbirth. It was believed that they developed from the fallen tail hairs of stallions or that they somehow formed spontaneously from the mud. Others believed that eels developed from eel slime itself, that they were sexless or emerged from the dew of May mornings, or even that to sleep with eels could ward off the plague.

Even now we know only some of the truth and their life remains one of the most glamorous in the natural world: an egg in the Sargasso Sea, a matchstick-sized elver crossing the oceans and ascending the rivers, a bootlace for years in the marsh, park pool, lake or reservoir, a mature fish at last, sensing the urge to mate, turning silver, feeling its digestive system atrophy, sensing the pull of the autumn moons and tides urging it to run in the blackest of nights from its resting place to the river, over all obstacles to the estuary, and on to the sea of its birth, where it will spawn and in its turn die – its extraordinary life cycle completed. As more and more anglers turn from the predictability of stocked fish, eels are bound to capture the imagination. No fish can be more truly wild, more a free spirit, and to understand them is to run with nature itself.

Not that any eel angler or eel researcher will ever claim to understand the fish entirely. In that alone, in their unknowability, eels represent one of the last major challenges of coarse fishing today. They are rarely visible and can remain half a century or more undetected in a pool and die without man ever guessing their presence.

Nor do we know why an eel is so rarely caught a second time. Almost certainly they do not die and equally surely they will never grace another man's landing net. Nor are we quite sure why some eels remain in freshwater and grow huge or which waters have the greatest potential. We have clues and good ideas even, but with the eel there are always continuing exceptions to confound any expert. I like to think I know a fair bit about river roach, Ritchie MacDonald knows most of what there is to know about pit carp and Derrick Amies has a pretty complete understanding of Broadland pike. Not even John Sidley or Brian Crawford, however, would claim to have more than a nodding acquaintance with the eel. Add this to the problems of hooking – and then landing – a big eel and you are looking at a lifetime's task. Indeed, it is probably true to say that there are many more eel hunters than there are big snakes landed.

LOCATION

The eel hunter in the 1990s faces more than one major problem in locating the big eel and one of them is created by man. For over twenty years now, the use of fyke nets for the commercial harvesting of eels stocks has been ever more prevalent. East Anglia I know intimately and I have seen the effect such netting can have. The nets can be laid by a man only semi-skilled, they are not very expensive to pick up second-hand and the netting licence fee is derisory. There are now many outlets for the man's catches and the payments are in cash and pretty well tax-free. The whole package looks attractive to the casual eel netter who is looking for a bit of beer money earned in a novel and intriguing way.

A young John Nunn with his fyke nets – one of the responsible men in the game.

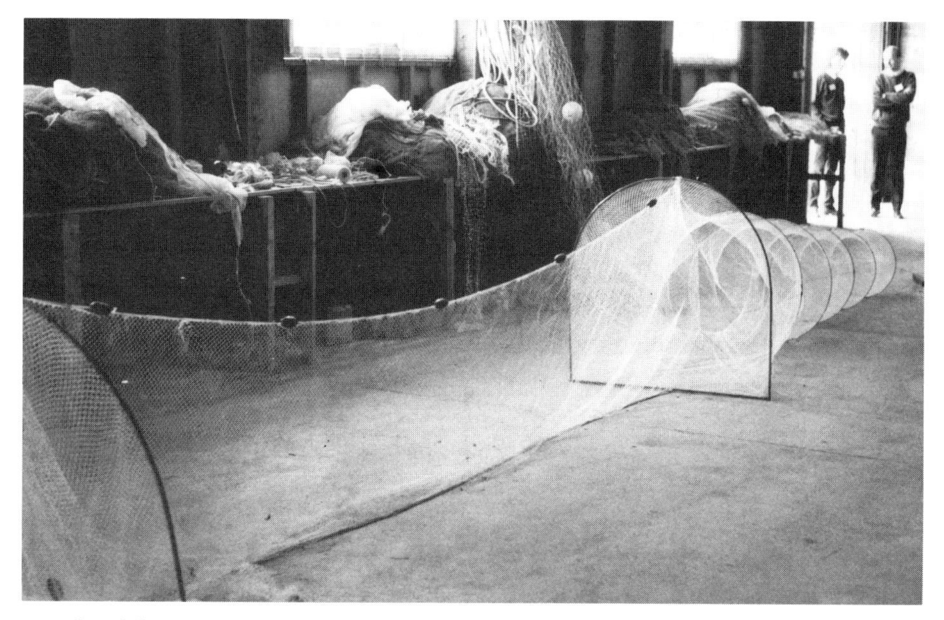

A mile of these can soon denude a water of eels.

So eel netting has probably generally been, but now at the other end of the scale is the professional man. I knew one in the 1970s and probably far more like him exist now. His operation was vast. During the summer-time he cruised the Broads with his team in a flotilla of cruisers and rowing boats. At night they laid down over a mile of fyke nets and their annual catch was in tens of tonnes. They claimed to be around 95 per cent effective on any water they visited and that did not leave many eels for the proper rod-and-line angler. Clearly, the presence of such men makes life for the big-eel angler truly difficult. Before anything else the angler must be sure that the water of his choice has not been netted in the recent past. If it has been, then his chances, never high, are reduced so massively that the water must be discounted. It is said that pike waters thrive on neglect. For eel waters neglect is a prime, essential factor.

The water must be an older, well established one. A 2lb eel will be over twenty years old and, presuming eels mature in the waters they entered as an elver, it is important to look at waters created before the 1960s. Ideally, then, the water should be a good way from the estuary and a long way up any watercourse. A water that produces big eels will probably hold few of them and the farther the elvers have to travel, the fewer of them will make it in the end. That old lake, miles from the river, irregularly fed by a rivulet in an old ditch, could be just the place – even if, especially if, no one knows of eels in the water. Should that rivulet then be totally blocked or destroyed by abstraction, so much the better. If the eels find it discouraging – or impossible – to leave a water then they will stay and grow into the specimens that big-fish anglers seek.

The 4lb-plus fish will very probably be a female and might be one of those very few fish that feel no mating urge. More likely, she will be a fish which did wish to run, to mate and to die but could not, for her way of escape was blocked. Perhaps she tried five, six even seven seasons to leave but, finding her exit denied, became infertile thereafter.

Moriarty, the leading eel researcher in Ireland, worked on a pond that had a housing estate built round it. The water's outlet was blocked and it became the archetypal prison water. There, Moriarty found enormous eels, many, many years old, which had been denied the Sargasso Sea and been doomed to a life of spinsterhood, growth and ease.

A water does not need to be connected to a river system at all – or even be near other water – to hold eels. In 1987 Roger Miller and I were told of a marlpit which held big perch. This pit is truly tiny, less than quarter of an acre. It is also on one of Norfolk's highest points – 100 feet up a flint and sand escarpment. The nearest watercourse of any description – and that only a very meagre stream – runs three-quarters of a mile away down the valley floor. And yet, on one of his earliest trips, Roger landed a 3lb 2oz eel from the place. How the fish had ever arrived there I cannot guess.

Having said all this about prison waters, the disturbing fact remains that very big eels have been caught from the most open of waters as well. The marshland dykes down the East Coast from Lincolnshire to Suffolk, which are only yards from the sea itself, have produced many eels over 5lb for those locals in the know. Rivers and canals hold large eels which have obviously made long-term homes for themselves in mill-pools, under weir aprons and around lock gates. Obviously these fish have easy, immediate access to the sea. Rumours of big eels in Loch Ness have existed now for over twenty years and their own return to the sea could not be easier. Draw, then, what conclusion you will!

Within a water, a few important factors should be noted. An eel likes to feel its body in contact with some solid substance – weed roots, earth, gravel, clay, mud, wood, old piping – and, therefore, will be found close to snags, to ledges, to islands, in gullies, by brickwork, wherever there are snags and cover. It is also true that eels frequently have living quarters and totally different feeding grounds, but it still makes sense to put a bait close to the areas where they spend most of their lives.

Rather like trout, it seems that eel populations have a definite pecking order and that the biggest eels secure the prime areas to live where they will be secure from intrusion from smaller fish. I remember John Wilson telling me after his diving experiences in local estate lakes that the very largest eels were holed up in the most densely snagged areas close to islands where fallen trees guarded their lairs. The smaller eels were found radiating outwards from the castle-like stronghold. Once more, such rulings are a simplification: big eels can be found in the most unexpected places in a water but it pays to play surer shots in a very long, waiting game.

TACKLE

When I was a child the anglers around me fished for eels with relatively crude tackle. That, though, was when there were fewer fyke nets on the waters and there were generally more eels to be caught. Today, large eels are comparatively rare and many have learned by being put back into the waters, sometimes by carp and tench anglers taking them on boilies. In essence,

An old marlpit – perfect hunting ground for crucians, rudd and the odd big old eel.

Bayfield Lake in its prime – then a fine eel water.

balanced tackle is the main aim. The rod, the line and the hook must be chosen to suit the conditions and be as light as possible, without running any risk of breaking off on a big fish. Like any specialist angler, an eel man will have a selection of rods to suit different conditions, waters, distances to be cast, baits, line and hooks to be used and size of fish to be encountered. There is no more a universal rod for eels than there is for carp. The rod, however, must be powerful and rarely is a test curve of under 2lb acceptable. Equally, reels must be totally reliable and have the capacity to take a large amount of heavier line. Mitchell 300s, Cardinals and Baitrunners are all excellent weapons in this respect.

Line strength itself is a problem on a new water and it is perhaps best to start with a realistic standard of 8lb BS. If there is evidence of very big fish or of serious snags this should be stepped up. If there are no takes then the line strength can be gradually brought down to a lighter 5 or 6lb perhaps, if the water is clear of snags. A hook trace will be necessary as the sharp teeth of an eel can easily sever nylon. Wire traces do present problems through their stiffness. Perhaps the new Kevlar traces marketed by Olympic will provide an answer. This material is virtually as soft as nylon and is coloured an unobtrusive green.

Hooks and swivels must be chosen equally carefully. Jack Hilton and Partridge hooks are as strong as any and are favoured by Brian Crawford. Hooks should be as small as the bait used allows. Berkley and Drennan swivels seem to be as strong as anything now on the market.

For years bite indicators were a most motley selection – silver-paper cylinders, pennies on the spool and a hubcap beneath, bent twigs and Heron alarms were all used with different levels of efficiency. Today there is little to beat the Optonics, with a Gardner-type drop-off system as back-up. Even Optonics can suffer either electric or battery failures and an undetected run can result in a deep-hooked and dead eel.

BAITS

Some eel waters seem to respond only to worms and small baits. On others only fish baits seem to work and there is a third category of water which will accept a mixture of the two approaches. To an extent, this difference seems to centre on the fact that some eel populations have broad heads and others have narrower, more pointed snouts. This phenomenon could well be a question of diet: those eels with the sharper heads possibly feed amongst weed, searching for various leeches, snails, caddis, shrimps, fish eggs and fry. They probably need a more delicate mouth to pick these up than the broader-headed eels, which are possibly fish eaters. The latter type develop bigger as well as broader heads, larger cheeks and sharper, bigger teeth. Possibly a young eel gets into a water, therefore, and develops in line with the food stocks of its home. There are problems with this thesis, of course. What, for example, happens to a long-lived broader-headed eel in a water where the small fish die off for some reason? Water dynamics are rarely stable over twenty years, never mind seventy, and presumably the eel has a capacity to adapt to changing circumstances. Still, these ideas appear decent ones and certainly it makes angling sense to match the bait to the water. As to which form of eel grows larger is once again open to debate. Initially it would seem that the fish eaters would do the better, eating larger nutritious prey. But, consider the effort a broad-headed eel has to put into the hunting of its food, compared with the easy life of a sharp-headed eel lying in the silt, sucking in daphnia, bloodworms and passing morsels.

Whichever water type is fished and whatever bait is used, it is imperative to spread as much smell as possible from the bait. Lobworms, for example, are best used in sections as the fractures allow more juices to spread through the water. The worms on the hook should be changed frequently. In the same way, the head sections of fish baits are good, especially if portions of the heart, liver and gut are attached. All coarse fish make good baits, perch especially if long casting is required. Small sections of trout, too, are excellent and appear to exude a rather different and enticing odour. Most sea fish make good baits – especially the smellier smelts, sardines and sprats. (The softer fish sections present a problem for longer casting and will have to be tied to the trace with PVA string.)

The question of aroma is central and the smell of the bait is obviously intensified if a feeder is placed from 9 – 12 inches up from the hook. This can be filled with cotton-wool pads soaked in high-smelling essences. Most smells are good, providing they are pungent: meat-based smells, squid, clam, mussel, crayfish, pilchard, ACE worm extract, even blue cheese and sweetcorn smells all work excellently. The only problem with the strongly scented feeder is that the eel might frequently take it rather than the intended bait. It makes further sense to fish this combination side on to the wind on the assumption that the smells will be carried by the underwater currents to the greatest number of eels possible. This can be a problem in the summer when the wind frequently dies at dusk, though some sort of undertow will probably remain for a while.

FROM RUN TO RETURN

When fishing the worm the strike should be made as quickly as possible, both to avoid deep hooking and to keep the eel away from immediate snags. It is possible to fish with worm with the rod up, barbel-style, with the hand ready on the butt for an instant strike. With larger fish baits and larger hooks the strike may be delayed for a few seconds, but the days of waiting for the second run are long gone and it is always better to pull out of an eel than to gut-hook it. If an eel comes in bleeding from the gills, then invariably it is a dead eel and may as well be killed and eaten rather than endure a lingering death. Eat, enjoy, feel ashamed and vow never to strike late again in the future. If a hook is in the side of the neck or the stomach even (God forbid), then cut the trace

Handling eels . . . Miller struggles for the knack.

as close as you can and it is possible that the eel will be able to deal with the hook itself. Barbless hooks, therefore, are an important consideration for the eel angler. Remember also that the days of whole fish baits are also in the past: fish sections need smaller hooks and again the strike can be a rapid one. Check that the line is running, tighten and hit it at once.

On the strike, try to hustle an eel away from snags. If the eel is large this will not be easy but hang on and pump. Try not to give line to an eel: it knows where it will go with it. Give an eel enough rope and it will hang you! At the same time, try not to hustle an eel to the net too quickly: a frantically fighting eel at this stage will pose massive problems. Keep the net sunk and try to get all the eel over the net before lifting. If the tail is over the side or the drawcord the eel will grip the frame and lever itself out of the net and the fight will begin again. If possible, give an eel over the net a fraction of slack and it should dive into the net of its own accord, thinking the net to be a snag. Altogether, the fight with a large eel is a ferocious affair. There is hardly a fish over 6 or 7lb that has not fought with unbelievable power. John Sidley has lost two fish estimated to be doubles that he was powerless to control.

Once netted, carry the eel well away from the water and do whatever you can in the net itself, as a naked eel is hard to hold. A lip-hooked eel – and most of them should be hooked there – can be freed with forceps. With anything deeper, clip the trace and sack the fish until the morning light. Then the eel can be laid on its back with a cloth over it to keep it steady. It will immediately calm down and the hook can be dealt with. Do not leave an eel in this position. Eels cannot breathe properly like this and their brain, too, is probably affected. Take photographs at this stage quickly and efficiently with a camera already set up and focused. Then – as all good eelers say – get that eel back alive.

The Record Eel Catch

John Sidley

No, I haven't broken the British eel record of 11lb 2oz set in 1978 by Stephen Terry from Kingfisher Lake in Hampshire, but I have done something as important in my own eyes. Readers of Brian Crawford's book, *Fishing for Big Eels*, will have read of the haul of twenty-three eels I made in one night at Westwood Park Great Lake in Droitwich. Those eels totalled 68lb 6oz with the best of the snakes just making 5lb. That was in my 1979–80 season and to the eel-angling world it was a haul of snakes that was mind-blowing for a one-night stint by a single angler. I certainly thought that the above target would never be equalled and yet on a Birmingham lake in my 1988–89 eel season I was to bank yet another single-night haul of eels which would and did shock the eel-angling brigade, myself included. I would now like to take you step by step through the stages of that unforgettable night.

The lake in question nestles on the outskirts of Birmingham and is called Upper Bittle reservoir. It is a top-up reservoir for the Stratford Canal and is owned by the British Waterways Board. It is some 90 acres in size when full and the Barnt Green Angling Club owns the fishing rights. Then, I was a new member of the club and the first to take serious note of the eeling potential of the lake. Certainly, it did not take me long to learn that there was a high population of eels in the venue. It was packed solidly with them.

Obviously, I began by locating the eels. Watercraft is, I feel, an important part of our fishing. Personally, I am not one for using echo sounders and I prefer to search out my venues by plumbing the depths and finding contours by rod and line. The most important element of all for me is walking the banks of all my waters and waiting for what I call the gut feeling to cry out at me. I feel that it is my instinct that says a particular swim holds eel or pike. Some anglers are gifted with this ability and over the years that I have been fishing, the feeling has helped me to catch some very big eels and pike. I simply pray that the gift will stay with me for ever.

Walking along the banks of Upper Bittle Reservoir, I soon came across an area of the lake which gave me this gut feeling and cried out to me, 'Snakes!'

Snags often mean eels.

There were no features such as weedbeds, gravel bars or sunken trees and all I was viewing was a bay that came off the main lake, known to the locals as Hopwood Arm. The only pointer was the amount of fish fry that had gathered into this one area. It was like finding a larder full of grub.

My next job was to start plumbing the depths with a rod and line with a pike float attached. I plumbed the bay, which was some 80 yards wide, and found that it ran from inches deep at the bank to 4 feet at the deepest. This was a channel that had been formed in heavy winter flooding by a feeder brook which ran into the lake at the bottom of the bay. In places the channel was only a foot or so wide but the good thing was that it was very heavily silted up with black mud. To me this again spelt snakes; it provided the perfect hiding place for eels to bury themselves while awaiting night to fall. Hiding away in this silted channel gave eels the protection they needed from herons and any hungry pike in the area. At the same time, the eels were smack bang in the middle of their feeding area. In short, if ever a swim cried out 'Eels!' then this one did.

Using one of the club's fishing boats, I placed a marker buoy in the channel. My next move was to start a prebaiting programme in the area, even though I felt that snakes were already present. I did, however, want to make doubly sure by giving them free meals. At the same time I hoped that I would get used

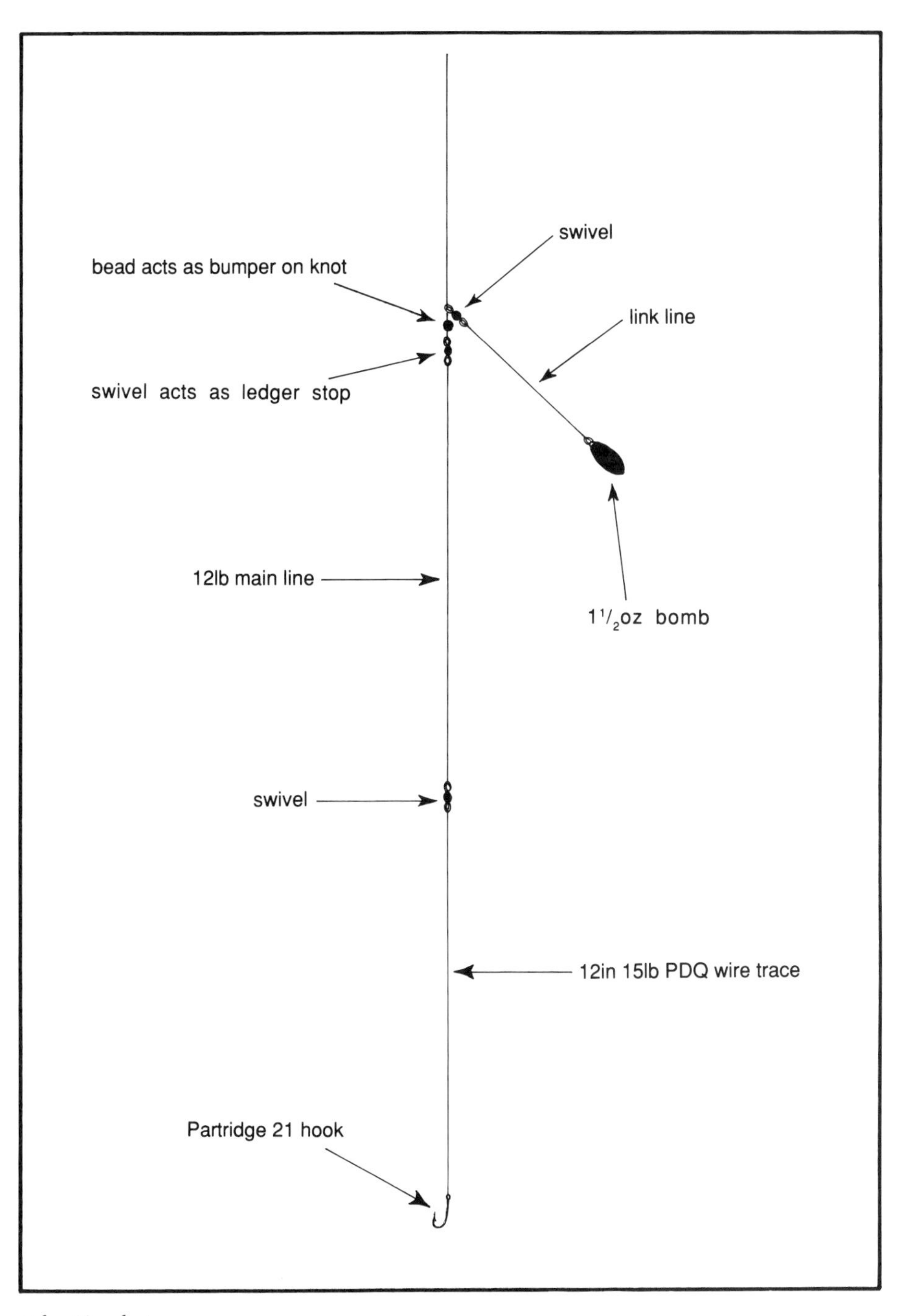

The JS eel rig.

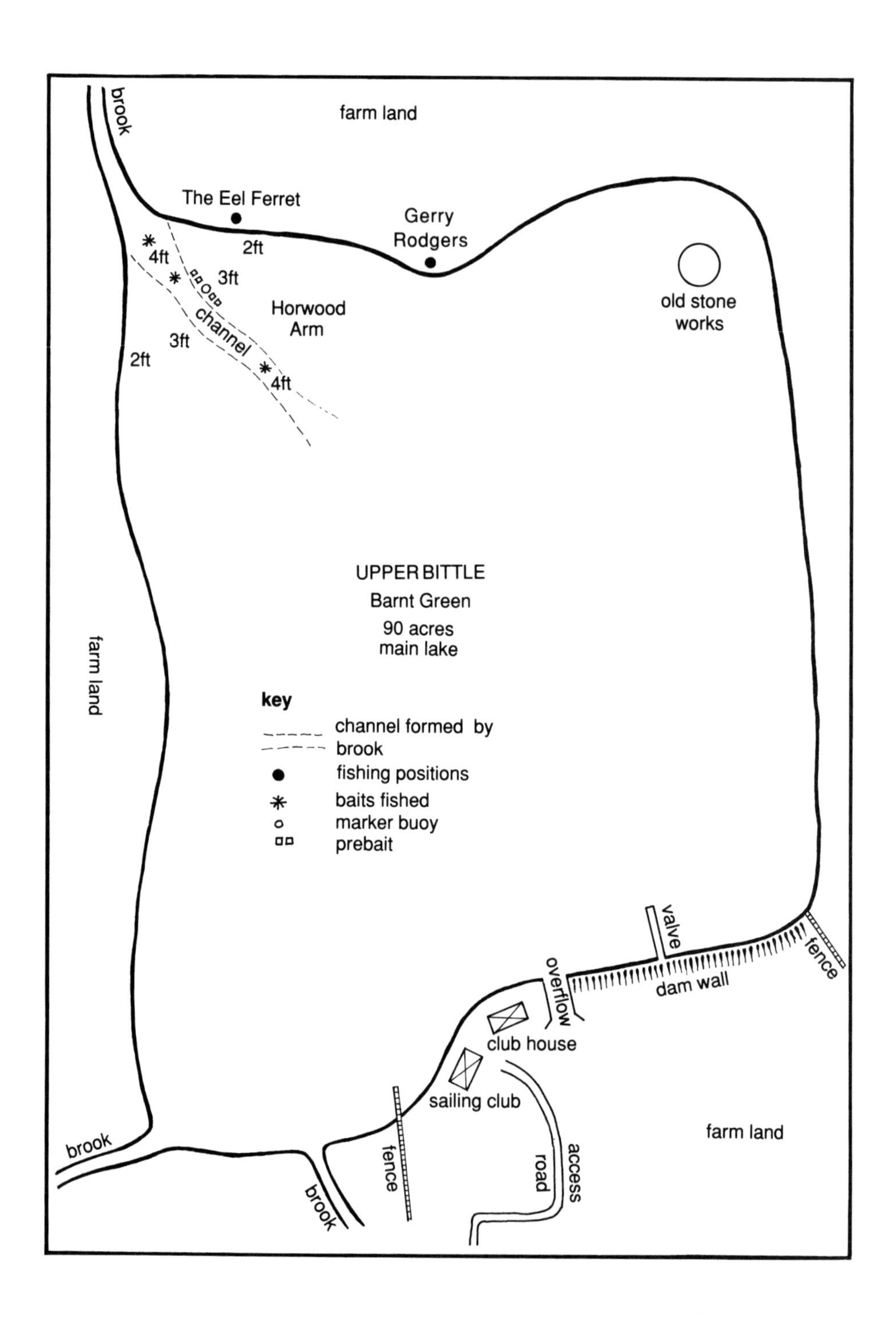
farm land
brook
The Eel Ferret
Gerry
Rodgers
2ft
4ft
3ft
Horwood
Arm
channel
3ft
2ft
4ft
old stone
works
UPPER BITTLE
Barnt Green
90 acres
main lake
farm land
key
channel formed by
brook
fishing positions
baits fished
marker buoy
prebait
valve
fence
overflow
dam wall
club house
sailing club
access
road
farm land
fence
brook
brook

to the baits I would be fishing on my hook. For two weeks before the season opened I spent every night going up to the swim and feeding it with Richworth sardines and sand eels. These were cut up into half-inch lengths. I was hoping that at these sizes the pike would not take too much interest in them, for experience told me that pikes and eels in the same swim do not mix.

My plan was to fish a sardine head on one rod and a sand eel head on the other. These would be ledgered hard on the bottom by means of the well-known JS eel rig. One rod would be the 12-foot Peter Drennan float pike rod and the other would be my own design, the JS eel rod. Reels were Mitchell 300s, loaded with 12lb Platil main line and a 15lb wire trace some 15 inches long. The hook was a size 8 Partridge and swivels were Drennan size 8s. An Optonic and monkey climber completed the set-up. A $1^1/_2$oz bomb ensured that I would get the baits into the channel.

On the head sections of bait the hook was positioned in the lips and on the tail sections the hook was inserted through the root of the tail itself.

All my homework done, I arrived at the car park of Upper Bittel Reservoir at 7.30 in the evening. Once again my fishing partner was Gerry Rodgers. While rowing over to our swim, Gerry said that he would fish the opening of the bay so that he would cover any snakes moving in or out from the main lake. We unloaded our gear and set about positioning ourselves in our chosen swims. The sardine head was cast out to the left of my marker buoy dead centre of the channel. I put the rod on its rests with the monkey climber in position and baited my second rod with a sand eel head. This was put out to the right of the marker buoy. My baits were now out and I sat on my deckchair and began to light up a cigarette and pour myself a cup of tea.

My mind wandered to past successes and failures as I awaited my first run. Then, without warning, both my Optonics sounded off together. The main line was leaving those reel spools at an alarming rate and I watched in horror as my monkey climbers shot up and down their needles for all they were worth.

I rushed-over to my first rod and then looked over at my second. I was unsure what to do. Panic took over. Still, I picked the first rod from its rests and wound down to a good snake. I felt my rod tip bang over and then the reel handle start to move in my hands. Right down through the rod I could feel the tell-tale thumps and that backing-off motion that only a sizeable eel can give. As quickly as I possibly could, I played my hooked eel to the bank. There was no time to net the fish so with care and luck I managed to beach it and drag it away from the water's edge. Now I was rushing over to my second rod to close the bail arm of the reel. I wound down for all I was worth. Once again the rod took on a healthy curve and a good battle took place before I could put my landing net under the second eel. Both were now unhooked

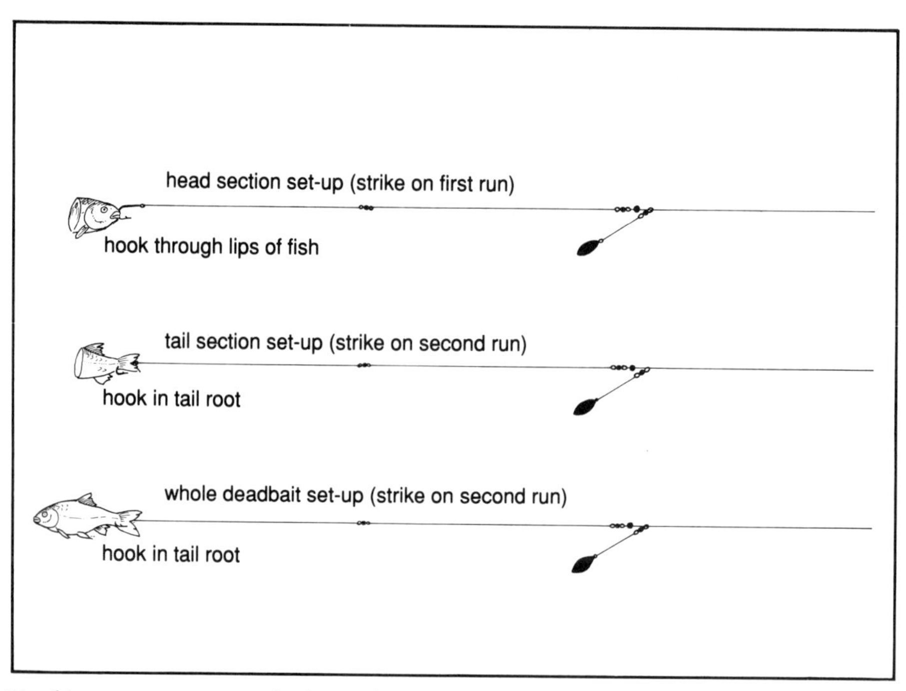

Hooking arrangements which are the same on both freshwater and sea deadbaits – such as sand eels, sardines and sprats.

and I placed each fish on my Avon scales. In the weigh sack the first eel went to 3lb 1oz and the second, 3lb 8oz. This was a great start and I hoped there was more to come.

All my prayers were answered and to write down everything that happened that night would fill the pages of this book. It was truly an eel angler's dream come true. Such was the action during that night that I was only able to fish with one rod. At times I cast my bait out into the channel near my marker buoy and had only started to sink my main line and put the rod on its rest when I felt the tip bang over to another taking eel. Never had I experienced this before.

When dawn broke over the lake the eel action had stopped because pike were moving to my bait. In all I landed nine pike with four of them going into double figures and the best weighing 14lb 14oz. By this time my angling friend Gerry was walking over to me.

Gerry asked me how I had got on during the night. I was speechless. All I could say was, 'Mate, you aren't going to believe this.' But believe it he did when he tried to lift out my keepnet. The sheer weight of the snakes inside made it impossible without fear of the net bursting. In fact it took the two of us to lift the haul clear of the lake. Gerry's comments I sadly cannot repeat. We both looked down at the incredible sight in my keepnet and both knew that I had a staggering eel catch there. After every eel was weighed and the pictures were taken we returned them all alive and well. All told, I had taken seven snakes over 1lb, sixteen over 2lb and nine over 3lb, with the best of the bunch going to 4lb. I dread to think what the final tally might have been if those pike had not moved in on my bait and pushed the eels out. As it was, the total weight was 86lb 13oz.

I remember leaving Upper Bittle Reservoir grinning like a Cheshire cat. Who could blame me? Gerry too was pleased enough for he took six eels, the best going one ounce over 4lb, before the pike moved in on his swim as well. So, there you have it – the full account of the biggest single night's haul of eels by one angler. On the right water the same or even better could happen again. All the angler needs is to know the feeding habit of the eel and to put the time and the effort into the venture. A comment I have made many times is that you will only get out of your fishing what you are prepared to put into it. The efforts I made studying the reservoir and choosing the swim and prebaiting it paid of handsomely. The catch was not a result of luck or being in the right swim at the right time. Never be fooled into thinking that eels are stupid and simply pull your rod in. They are not. They are as cunning as any big carp, tench, bream or pike, so give them credit. On your next eeling stint take the time to walk right round the lake and do not just drop into a swim because somebody you know took a good eel from it the previous week. Work on your own watercraft and develop the gut feeling that must be inside you. If you do these things, who knows what your next stint could give you? Perhaps you, too, will have a night to remember.

NOTE This catch of thirty-three eels taken by John was confirmed by the National Anguilla Club and the British Eel Anglers Club as being the biggest single night's haul of eels ever taken by one angler in a single fishing session. Out of interest, sixteen of the eels fell to sardine-head and seventeen fell to sand-eel-head bait.

The Eel Campaign

Mick Brown

A serious eel campaign is not to be taken lightly for it can place demands on one's family life, health, work and, indeed, sanity itself. An idea turns into a campaign and the campaign becomes an obsession in the tired mind of the eel angler. Endless sleepless nights take their toll. Many campaigns are terminated prematurely. Sometimes the reason is an early success but most often despondency and disillusion creep in and the plan is not adhered to or other, easier targets become a distraction. Worse still, the big-eel fanatic can fall into the trap of thinking that his quarry is the only fish worth pursuing during the summer months and thoughts of them burrow deep into his mind. Summer nights at home in bed seem uneasy, restless affairs as one's mind drifts far away to dark eerie places that no sane person would visit on his own in the middle of the night. Images of huge, writhing predators entangled in tree roots and sunken branches never leave one's thoughts.

How does an angler get himself into such a state of mind? Well, everything has its beginnings, and encounters with small eels in my formative years had fuelled the fire that was going to rage in seasons to come. As a youngster, eels to me were just a nuisance which kept taking my baits intended for trout on the Welsh streams during the spring and summer. They weren't particular, either. Be it minnows, worms, cheese or maggot on the hook, they would take it. In later years they became a close-season diversion as we realized that by adhering to certain rules we could carry on fishing after 14 March. Happy, innocent days with only one rod apiece and a bucket of worms between us. Later still the eel was to become the target species of budding specimen hunters like myself. Anglers such as Bob Church started to make a name for themselves with the species and, as if they were previously unknown, stillwaters became the focus of the big-eel anglers' attention. About this time, 1968, I was invited to join the ranks of the South Staffordshire Specimen Group, whose members at that time included Joe Day, the one-time barbel record holder. We also had a young lad named Des Taylor join us for a while. I wonder what happened to him. In those days, three-pound eels were regarded as big fish and even two-pounders were highlighted in red in the group record book. How times change! With ever-improving communications and transport, it is now easily possible for the enlightened eel man to take half a dozen such fish in a single night from a multitude of waters which had not been fully exploited in the past. As for 4lb-plus fish, in those days they were rare and indeed that situation has not changed much to this day, and many quite experienced eel anglers have yet to net such a fish. One thing never changes: the biggest eels are nearly always caught by accident, often by an inexperienced young angler fishing for something else. Very frustrating when your own efforts have produced very little of late, but at least it proves that eels are there to be caught.

Eels do not show themselves to the same extent as the majority of other species so the most important matter of location can be very difficult. Once eels are located, fishing for them is a relatively simple matter in terms of tackle and techniques though actually putting them on the bank can be quite another thing. Nowadays the angling grapevine is buzzing with news of good eel waters but in those days this was not so and location was a long, hard business, often a question of trial and error. As in all procedures there had to be a learning curve and in retrospect we made a lot of mistakes by sticking on the wrong waters. This did not detract from the pleasure and intense anticipation

One of Mick Brown's early successes.

that we enjoyed. For a couple of seasons the group record crept up to a – then good – fish of 3lb 7oz, which fell to my rod.

Then, one damp June night, it happened. An eel latched on to my multiple-worm bait which was to be the cause of endless restless sleepless nights. Under cover of darkness a young man armed with two rods, a sack and a big landing net climbed over a fence to enter the grounds of a city-centre park which was strictly closed to the public at night. Police with dogs ensured that this was adhered to. The reason for this clandestine visit was that I had heard that carp anglers fishing the park pool were regularly being bitten off when they were fishing worm baits over bubbling fish. Such rumours require investigation by the eel angler. Two huge balls of worms were freelined into what was really an uninspired choice of swim on a hitherto unknown water. Rods were simply laid on the concrete-sided bank and pieces of aluminium foil looped over the line as a means of bite indication. A far cry indeed from my present day set-up, with multiple Optonics and monkey climbers on a rod pod!

I vividly recall the carp rolling beneath the rod tips while I resisted the temptation to catch them as I feared that the resulting disturbance would reduce to nil my chances of an eel. Yet my decision proved to be right when an hour later the right-hand indicator started to scrape along the concrete path and then stopped – an electrifying sound in the stillness of the night. I pulled it back into position but within seconds it started to creep along again and then stopped. This little game went on for quite a few minutes and then I decided to strike and investigate. The next thing I remember was being attached to something that seemed intent on pulling my arms from their sockets. To latch on to a good eel at close range is a memory never to be forgotten. For an indeterminate time the brute just pulled and pulled and pulled. Never moving to left or right, it just paddled backwards in a solid, pounding resistance. Gaining inches at a time, I finally won the battle and ran well away from the water's edge with my prize, a 39 ¾-inch-long eel weighing 5lb 8oz and firmly hooked in the top lip.

I'd found a good eel water at last but, as it was strictly closed after dark, how was I ever going to exploit it? For three frustrating years I occasionally climbed over that fence, either to be chased out or to fish badly as a result of looking over my shoulder all the time. To add my frustration, I also heard of more eels biting off the carp anglers' hooks. My break came along, more by luck than anything else when, at a carp syndicate meeting, I overheard someone mention that some other anglers had actually got permission to fish some of the city parks at night. If they could get permission, perhaps I could too. The South Staffs Specimen Group had since been disbanded but, using some old headed paper with the group name on it, I sent a letter to the local

A huge eel for the young Mick Brown.

council responsible for the water and described an elaborate project that I wished to carry out there. I was quite open when I expressed my deep desire to study the water and its eel potential, which could only be done at night. Never expecting more than a polite reply, I came out in a hot sweat when one morning I opened a letter laying out the conditions of my being allowed to fish there during the coming summer.

Things were falling into place in many ways in my life. This would be my last summer of total freedom as I was planning to get married the following spring. Now, serious eel fishing is a very selfish business as continual night fishing means that during the daytime you feel unfit for anything else.

I'm not talking about dozing soundly in a bivvy all night, but real fishing where you are continually tending and altering your tackle throughout the session. Your work can suffer and so can your social life. Stephanie, my girlfriend, was understanding in the extreme and we decided that this would be my final fling before we settled down. The hunt would soon be on.

Also around this time, I became involved in a career development scheme. Normally I had to go into the office neat and tidy and wearing a suit. For this summer I could go in jeans and a T-shirt as I was to exchange places with an engineering graduate at a local research centre. The work was highly technical but at times very dirty, so formal clothing was excused. Ideal for someone who had been out all night and had no time to get properly cleaned up.

June the sixteenth was getting closer and closer. My permit was only to last until September so I had to plan properly and get it right. First of all I visited the water in daytime and made a detailed plan of every feature of note. The water was only about two acres or so and its long thin shape meant that I could cast to every square yard of it. I sketched a rough map out and marked on it all the features that could be of significance. There were two islands, one large and one small, a moored boat with two heavy anchor chains and an ornamental fountain and underwater pipework supplying it. Not so obvious were the bottom contours and features. The end which took the force of the prevailing wind was thick with mud from years of decaying leaves and other debris. Elsewhere the bottom was generally hard, with two deep holes adjacent to the two islands. Depth is a relative term and these holes were only about six feet deep in a pool averaging about three feet. I assumed that the designers of this man-made pool had planned these features for the fish to overwinter in should the weather turn severely cold. Another feature that interested me was the way the branches from the tree-laden islands hung well over and into the water in places. Beneath the surface they intermingled with their own roots and fallen branches – a very interesting and potential holding feature in a water that was, during the daytime, as noisy as a fairground.

I next divided my map into fourteen sections of roughly equal size. My intention was to spend time in each one until a pattern emerged. This would prevent me from being influenced by particular features and spending all my time in just one or two swims and possibly missing something.

The first night finally arrived. With intense anticipation I set off through the noisy city streets to be ready for the midnight start. On arrival I slowly climbed over the low fence at the front instead of struggling over the high fence at the back, knowing that if challenged I needn't run this time – a comfortable, smug feeling. I headed, of course, for the swim where I'd taken the $5^1/_2$ pounder, even though that fish was no longer in the pool. My inexperience had resulted in my putting the eel into another pool after photographing it at home. I moved my baits a few times but daybreak loomed all too soon to reveal a cold, tired angler who had no sign of a run despite the perfect conditions.

My style of fishing has always been to go and find some fish rather than wait for them to find my baits and with the small amount of tackle that I take eel fishing with me regular moves are no problem. As I like to stay awake and fish, as opposed to waking to strike a run, I don't need much more than the basic tackle. All I take apart from my rods and net is a small rucksack with the few bits and pieces I'll need and a plastic-covered piece of foam rubber to sit on. Travelling light proved to be essential in the park grounds anyway, as approaching gangs of drunks and yobs had to be avoided from time to time.

That night had been peaceful, but with no sign of fish of any sort whatsoever I'd spent five fishless hours at one end of the pool and the logical thing to do seemed to be to move to the opposite end for the remaining few hours until I had to go.

This was more like it. The surface scum that had accumulated at this end was alive with dimpling fish. The occasional carp showed itself and bubbling fish were in evidence everywhere. A good move had definitely been made. My eye was also caught by groups of small fish scattering. Very often two or three different groups would scatter at the time – very interesting in a pool that contained no other predators except eels. The bubbles interested me in

A heavily weeded but still fishable lake – eels adore weed and tree roots.

particular and I carefully lowered a bunch of lobs into a small patch within inches of the concrete bank. I stood silently in the early morning half-light and waited to see what would happen. For five minutes nothing did and so I decided to lift the bait and see if it was covered in leaves. As I lifted it I became aware that something strange was happening and I realized that an eel, of ample proportions, was hanging on to the worms. It only let go when its head was several inches out of the murky water, which at that point was only about a foot deep. I'd just missed a very good fish.

Time was ticking away and I soon had to start thinking about work so without hesitation I tackled another set of bubbles in one of the areas where the small fish had been scattering. After a long wait my worms remained untouched and I was concerned that the leaves and bottom debris were so dense that even a feeding eel might overlook them. The line suddenly tightened, only a few inches or so, and striking was an instinctive reaction as opposed to a thoughtful decision. Wow, these eels can't half pull at close range! The water erupted into a stinking black mess as the writhing specimen churned up years and years of accumulated debris. Many minutes later a 4lb 11oz eel was in the net and spewing up the small perch that it had been feeding on.

A lovely summer pond where big eels hide in the brickwork of the dam.

A very tired but pleased angler set off in the early morning sunlight to get cleaned up for work.

Two nights later I returned for another session. I was thinking about those fish that the eels were taking and decided that deadbaiting should be the next line of attack. The eels hadn't got particularly big mouths but they had proved to be fish eaters. About that time I had just discovered a good way of getting a few livebaits from this type of water. It involved simply scooping around the deeper margins with a large landing net; with a bit of practice and stealth a few small fish could easily be obtained. Very quick and effective. I never ever took baits with me to this pool as within ten minutes I could always get half a dozen small roach, which was as many as would ever be needed.

Deadbaiting produced an instant success for at one o'clock that night I was away on a five-inch roach that I'd cast against the mooring chain of the large boat anchored there. After a hell of a tussle a 4lb 1oz eel was tasting the warm night air. At 35 inches long it was, like the other two, as fat as a rolling-pin.

Could such luck continue? The answer was yes and a few more blanks were punctuated by two moments of sheer bliss. The first was in the form of a 4lb 3oz eel caught on a deadbait against the large island and the second was a long, thin specimen of 4lb 9oz taken on a link-ledgered bunch of brandlings against the small island. Moving around the pool seemed to be paying off, with no particular swim being the hot area.

A series of blanks followed. You can't just pull out big eels indefinitely and the action had to slow down at some time. The problem is getting your brain to understand this and inevitably I kept going at it. The strain of all those lost nights of sleep started to show. At work I became known as 'the eel man' as the others there began to find out about my nocturnal habits. I'm sure that they thought I was crazy. For a time I probably was. My eyes became black and sunken and one morning I overheard my boss saying how ill I looked. The truth was that I really did feel ill. Some of the work that I was involved in was quite hot and at times quite physical and after a night out eeling it became an exhausting business. One morning I went into the toilets at nine o'clock just to rest my legs and eyes for a few minutes. I remember waking up four hours later to the sound of my colleagues washing their hands for the lunch-hour break. Something had to be done and so occasionally I took a bed-chair and blanket with me, but to be quite honest the excitement just wasn't the same as being over the rods when the indicator started to move.

Among numerous blanks, the next two eels went 3lb 2oz and 3lb 10oz to worm baits in heavily baited swims – good eels, but almost insignificant after the previous encounters. Some nights I fought off the tiredness just to follow an impulse to put a bait in a certain spot. My tired mind was in overdrive trying

Selbrigg Pond – a once-famous eel and rudd pond.

to find a way of latching on to another of those fabulous fish. Most of those summer nights were spent walking round without any shoes on as many of the eels were feeding very close to the bankside. Those nights were full of so many memories, some magical and others less so. Occasionally I would be shaken from my slumber by a rat or hedgehog scurrying through my tackle. On other occasions I would have the company of a couple of foxes, which would hunt the margins for dead fish. I often used to leave fish out for them to take. As though without legs, they would drift to the water's edge and then, at the slightest movement from me, would melt away again in a silent gallop.

Then there was the old tramp. Looking over sixty years old but probably not much more than forty-five, he bent my ear for many a night. I didn't mind hearing about his unhappy past but I wished he wouldn't keep throwing those cider bottles into my swim! What with him living in the rhododendron bushes nearby on the one hand and the haunted house behind me on the other, can you wonder that I didn't get much sleep?

The haunted house stories would take up a chapter on their own. Were the things that I saw and heard the product of a tired mind? One night I watched another angler arrive about a hundred yards away from where I was fishing.

He was clearly illuminated by the lights of a nearby building and apparently he had not noticed me sitting under the cover of a large tree. This was, to say the least, an unusual event as the security patrols were thorough and frequent. I admired his nerve, having done the same myself in the past, and gave him time to tackle up before I went down to chat with him and compare notes. As I approached, something strange was happening. I suddenly became aware that I couldn't see him any more. With apprehension I got closer. There was no sign of angler or tackle yet for him to pack up his gear and go would have taken quite a while. I broke out in a cold sweat and I'm sure that my hair stood on end. Five minutes later I was driving home.

August came round and holiday commitments meant that I didn't fish the pool for two weeks. The obsession was really biting and no matter what else I was involved in during the holiday my mind was filled with thoughts of catching those eels. Should I try this swim? How about this bait? What about this method? I was, at times, wishing that I could just walk away from it and lead a normal life as all my other mates did. Luckily for me, Steph was understanding and stuck by me through it all – the best friend that I ever had but, sadly, no longer with us in this world. As darkness approached on each chosen night I could always rely on my flask and food being ready. A tired,

Steering a big fish from the lilies.

restless angler needs a lot of understanding. On many occasions I just couldn't stay awake during the evening and often fell into a deep sleep. On one occasion I jumped up, frightening Steph out of her wits, as I shouted out for a landing net. Crazy days!

The holiday break probably did me a power of good and with September fast approaching my batteries were well recharged for the final onslaught. Although worm had produced some very good fish, I decided to deadbait mainly from now on to avoid the nuisance runs that I was getting on worms from other fish. The disturbance, I felt, may have been scaring away the eels and also the frequency of these twitch-type bites was responsible for stopping me getting at least a little rest.

While I had been away one of the local carp anglers had done a bit of poaching at night in one of the island swims. He came down several times while I was fishing and on one occasion told me that while using worm for bait, over many visits, he had landed a 2½lb eel and had been bitten off twice. Very interesting. He was obviously not using wire traces and with such big eels about in a snaggy swim the result was inevitable. Using wire I had landed six out of six but I was mindful of the fact that fishing light and without a trace might produce more runs. I was almost tempted that night to dispense with wire but memories of some of the battles I'd had with those previous eels prevented me from doing so.

On one particular night my friend had stayed and chatted to me until about one o'clock. Shortly after he had left, and with another pleasant night ahead of me, I decided that a cup of tea was in order. Before I could reach for the flask I noticed that one of my indicators had moved a little. Were those rats responsible again? No, not this time, for I was away on a small island. In the still of the night a right hauling competition took place. The rod bucked and the line whipped from side to side through the still air and I winced at the feel of the line grinding and grating among the unseen snags. The only thing to do was walk backwards, gaining inches at a time, for turning the reel under such pressure was simply out of the question. Minutes later and with luck still at my side, the eel was away from the snags but still dragging something with it. As it approached the landing net I was horrified to see in the torch beam that the eel was attached to a 4 foot-long branch, waterlogged and blackened after years beneath the water.

The next few seconds could best be described as a ridiculous spectacle but in retrospect I could have done nothing else. The eel obviously wouldn't go in the net but I did try. With the eel half in and the whole lot getting into a worse and worse mess all I could do was throw the rod to one side and grab the eel, net and branch and throw the lot up on the bank behind me. What a tangle!

The eel was sacked and meanwhile I stopped shaking. The next morning it was weighed and measured at 5lb 11oz – a very fat eel exactly 40 inches long. Words are insufficient to describe these moments and I won't even try.

The end of summer was approaching and the project was nearing its end as my permit was soon to run out. A long-suffering Steph stuck by me to the end, when I'm sure most women would have had enough. It must have been my good looks and personality! The last sessions, predictable, produced a lot of blanks and just one more eel, which, although not the biggest, remains most firmly in my memory. I only wish that I had the ability to put into words the atmosphere of nights like the one when I caught this last eel. The best of the summer was over and the nights were getting longer and colder. Dog-tired, but loving every minute of it, I lay, wrapped in an old army blanket, in the damp grass, cropped short by the grazing Canada geese. No thoughts of fame, fortune or publicity crossed my mind. All that I wanted was to feel the rod buck over violently as a big eel pulled back in the blackness of the night. At a quarter past three that night my wish came true. A flyer of a run on two lobs was met with some sort of strike as a weary but excited angler fumbled with the rod and moving line. It was on and gave the best fight of the lot. Pounding away relentlessly in the chilly night, the eel finally gave way to my efforts. That moment still burns in my memory. My back was aching and my bare feet squelched in the mud and droppings at the water's edge. Late-night traffic rumbled by in the distance and the whole world was unaware of me unhooking that lip-hooked 4lb 2oz bronze-coloured beauty – a lovely eel in every way.

I weighed it and, in a split-second decision, decided that it should not be kept from the water any longer. For a while I even questioned what right I had to have removed it in the first place. The feeling passed and without measuring, photographing or further ceremony the eel disappeared back into the murky water. I doubt whether many people, even some anglers, can see the sense in going to all that trouble to catch a good fish and then slip it straight back. I don't look for sense or reason and purely allow my instincts to tell me what is right.

September came round and I sent my report in to the council department that had issued my permit. I wondered what those non-anglers thought of it. Twenty-eight all-night sessions for eight eels averaging 4lb 4oz in weight. A waste of time? I think not.

Oddities

There are many fish species that are out of the mainstream of normal angling and yet they are all likely, excepting one, to be met by the serious angler once or twice in a long career. They all merit attention as beautiful or interesting creatures. In fact, many of the fish that I will now describe are worth actively seeking out and pursuing.

BURBOT

I doubt whether any reader of this book will have seen or indeed will ever see a burbot – 'these strange creatures, half fish and half eel, which we of the fens call eel-pouts and the book naturalist call burbots. A sort of lamprey with suckers on top of their heads' (J. Wentworth Day, *A History of the Fens*).

Burbot are, or were, not strictly stillwater fish but more inhabitants of the slow rivers, drains and dykes of Durham, Lincolnshire, Yorkshire, Cambridgeshire and all of East Anglia. However, as many of these waters could not muster the breath to move a float, I think that the burbot's inclusion is fair. Until even the middle of this century, though often localized, they were common fish that weighed up to 2–3 lb and could be caught quite easily by all usual methods and baits. As late as 1954, Wentworth Day could write:

> That hideous looking fish the eel-pout or burbot is common enough in the upper waters of the Ouse and in the Cam and Burwell Lode where I caught it when tickling tench. It usually clings close to the bank. Eel-pouts used to abound in my fen, sometimes up to three pounds in weight; this odd fish has a flat head, a big mouth, bulging shoulders, three feelers, one over each eye and one under the chin. They eat frogs, beetles, crayfish and even small water rats. But I do not advise anyone to eat them. The taste is filthy.

Yet even as he wrote, the days of the burbot were numbered and the last properly credited specimen caught on rod and line seems to have been landed in 1969 on the River Ouse. Attempts have been made since then to locate and

Once home to the burbot . . . the dykes and drains of East Anglia.

land this strange little fish and Richard Walker led a strong team to try to prove their continued existence. He failed. Around that time the *Angling Times* put up a large prize for any verified rod-caught burbot but to this day the money rests safe.

It is not hard to obtain advice about the fish as plenty of old-timers still living in the fens and East Anglia remember the burbot well and with not a little nostalgia. A warm, muggy summer evening would seem to be favourite, with a good-sized worm ledgered hard in to the bank of reeds and rushes. Every man I have talked to had his own favourite river, dyke or broad so the swim should not be a problem if they still exist, which they probably do not. What makes me sure of this is that East Anglia is now very thoroughly eel-netted and, as far as I can make out, it is many years since even a fyke net last contained a burbot. Sadly, I feel, we have to conclude that the burbot is no longer with us.

Quite why is open to debate. It seems that the general run-down in the quality of the environment, and especially recent wetland drainage schemes, proves to be incompatible with this long-established creature. If only eel-pouts were beautiful, feathered creatures rather than ugly silt dwellers, then the public opinion would have risen in fury long ago. As it is, only we anglers can praise the burbot. As well as bury him. There have been rumours of burbot pockets, many of which I have followed up, in the past fifteen years. All have proved disappointing. Yarmouth marshes, Wells marshes, the Babingley river, the Wissey and even the Thurne have all been investigated and proved barren. Eels, lampreys or simple imaginings have proved to be at the base of the rumours and I suspect that it is only abroad that the burbot can still be found.

SILVER BREAM

The number of people to fish specially for silver bream now or in the past must be minute and yet I cannot but feel that they deserve a mention here. The first bream that most young anglers landed would have been be an 8 or 12oz silver with an eye and an appetite too big for its own good. No one has ever doubted that they are pretty fish but, rarely exceeding 1lb in weight, they are not the stuff of more adult dreams.

Indeed, the record now remains vacant at 2lb or so. It seems that even if a 'big' silver is caught the lucky captor cannot be bothered to weigh it. It is better, apparently, not to be in the hall of fame at all than to enter on the back of a silver bream.

All this is a shame for, like many species, the silver bream is in decline and soon, like the burbot, could be a fish of the past. Traditionally, it has lived in English Eastern counties, north of the Thames. Lincolnshire, the Fens, the Cam, the Great Ouse systems and broadland have been the prime silver areas and recent changes in the aquatic environment are definitely thinning out numbers quickly.

Yet there still remain big ones to be caught. In 1986 I heard of a silver nudging 3lb taken from a Norfolk boat dyke but the captor returned it feeling it could be a common bream. I saw the photograph and remain convinced he did land a record silver that day. The pharyngeal teeth of the two species do differ: the silver's are arranged in two series – more obviously when adult – the silver is less slimy than the common bream, more slender across the back and in depth, has a comparatively larger eye and is, of course, very decidedly silver in colouring on the flanks, with a green-tinted back.

Like his bigger cousin, the silver is hardly renowned for his reel-screeching runs but that does not mean he is not worth following up if you get a whiff on him. He is caught readily on maggots, brandlings and bread and lives in good-sized shoals. On a recent trip to a large European river, in five casts I caught five silver bream, every one of which would have broken the English record. They all fought well and looked quite lovely together for a short while on wet sacking before being released – to the fury of the Continentals, who eat virtually everything that swims.

In England, if I really wanted to emulate this feat, I would poke around fenland or broadland boat dykes in the winter. I think the chances of smashing the present lowly record qualifying weight are high. But who wants fame to such a great degree?

CRUCIAN CARP

Crucians are of course not oddities. I must say this at once before I have the country's number one crucian carp expert, Bernie Neave, after me with a hatchet. Still, I do think they are queer, very peculiar indeed in both how they

Bernie Neave – crucian slayer – into his favourite fish.

look and how they behave. It is certainly hard to improve on what Bernie has already written on the species in *Carp – The Quest for The Queen* (second edition), but I feel that things can be added.

In his chapter in that book Bernie describes crucians as adorable, hunky, chunky fish, and with all this I agree. But they also possess the characteristic of no other species – a sense of humour. This too shows in their faces. These are fat, roly-poly characters whose eyes twinkle and little barbuleless mouths are curled into perpetual grins. These are smug enough to become sneers at half a chance – and there are plenty of those!

Bernie has made notable steps forward in the art of crucian fishing. Dawn sessions, flavoured groundbaits, delicate float settings and bait presentation are all vital steps in the game for this incredibly wily small fish and we are all indebted to Bernie for the inroads he has made. However, as usual, I have spent several sessions after crucians this summer and , while I have found them no less baffling, one or two more answers have transpired.

The first point of interest occurred when I was actually watching Bernie practise his art one morning early in June. The weather was typically hot and sunny and the water had already shrunk considerably because of agricultural abstraction around the lake. As the sun rose higher I saw what I had never

The eternal beauty of a summer stillwater.

done before – crucian carp feeding in the swim. They fed every bit as you would expect, very like tench, their larger carp cousins, hovering, tipping up, hoovering in a few particles and then hanging horizontal again while chewing them. The whole process was very relaxed and gentle and the whole shoal was in a tight circumference of about three or four yards.

A point of major interest is that all the feeding crucians kept in the shade thrown by an alder tree and, what is more, they never deserted that shade as the sun moved. Repeatedly in the next few weeks I found that fishing hard into trees, bridges, boathouses and other shade-casters improved my catches.

It was also noticeable that if Bernie struck at a bite and missed the whole shoal of crucians was immediately disturbed, would scatter for a couple of minutes and only begin feeding again with caution. Of course, you always have to strike at a bite but I made quite sure thereafter that I only struck at definite bites and that I did not strike wildly. I stopped even striking at the end of a cast, as so many anglers do out of habit. In fact I did everything possible to ensure that the swim was as little disturbed by my tackle as I could manage. Casting over distance and slowly retrieving to the correct spot was, of course, an automatic thing to do.

My final and major breakthrough was to understand the huge importance of night fishing for crucians. Because crucians are small it is easy to forget they are part of the carp family and possess every bit of the wariness and intelligence of their larger cousins. Clever groundbaiting, delicate presentation and fine tackle are not always enough for older fish that have seen a fair bit of angling pressure over the years. This was brought home to me by tales from the local pit where fish from 2 to $2^1/_2$lb were being taken from 11 p.m. to 4 a.m. in June. My own crucian water was proving just about impossible, it seemed, with only a single success – admittedly a big fish – in some eleven sessions. In August I got back to them with all the equipment for night fishing and in three sessions landed eight fish, losing a ninth at the net.

Little has been said about the existence of crucian x carp hybrids in the past. I have examined several photographs of big 'crucians' over the last few years and it is a sad fact that many of these fish were in fact crosses. Their mouths might have been right (with no barbules) but their heads and bodies were the wrong shape or their scales seemed slightly too large. Before claiming a big crucian, do check that you have exactly the right product in front of you. On this point, does anybody know what a prussian carp is? The old books and indeed an old print I possess frequently mention them as a crucian subspecies. They look slimmer and perhaps were wild carp x crucian crosses that achieved official status in the old biology books.

A rare grass carp success.

GRASS CARP

As the proud captor of only two grass carp I feel utterly ill-equipped to add much on the species in this country. All I can do is to reinforce the case for stocking them as a species of beauty, great interest and fighting ability.

My only British grass carp came from a small pond, so badly coloured that I could only just make out the shapes in the water and certainly could not make out the species. I guessed at chub, or common carp, but I had no bait with me and could not get the fish to the surface to make sure. Then it was that a thistle head broke off, fell into the water and drifted out before the wind. After only a few yards, a head emerged and engulfed it in a great swirl with fleshy lips. Now it was my turn to send out a broken reed and watch that similarly disappear. All I had with me was fly tackle, but a stripped hook and three inches of reed did, as they say, the business in the shape of a 3 or 4lb grass carp that fought manically and looked quite beautiful in the sunlight. It glowed a luminous pearl colour, which I found quite enchanting.

My other grass carp came from the flood plain of a great southern European river. In winter and spring the river presumably floods widely but in the summer it shrinks back to leave little pools isolated and land-locked. In one of these, no more than twenty-five yards long and less than half that in width, I came across my second grass carp – this time about twice the size and just as beautiful. I returned at dawn the next day on the strength of just a suspicion of a fish I had seen in the murky waters.

The beauty of that emerging day was quite staggering as the sun rose through its mists to dazzle on the fields of corn, white church spires, and the wide blue river a dozen yards behind me. But it was the fish by my float that riveted my gaze. From the gentle steaming water a grass carp between 25 and 30lb rolled over my corn. Some five minutes later the float disappeared and I am sad to say that I was broken by a fish that I just could not keep from the jungle of undergrowth which had fallen into the water opposite.

A grass carp of dreams.

KOI CARP

My koi carp record is just as feeble – more so, in fact – and rests on just a single fish that I came to know very well indeed. I happened to be fishing the small lake in the grounds of a recently deceased angler's house. In the late-March afternoon, I landed a quite brilliantly coloured koi carp. As the house and lake were about to be sold and as I had just purchased a house with two lakes that I was stocking, the angler's widow suggested that I take this nugget of a fish home with me. This I did and for the next seven years I kept a close watch on him. He grew a fair bit, kept his fabulous colours but, interestingly, was only caught once again despite quite heavy fishing pressure and a relatively limited water area to escape in. His wariness contrasted strongly with the comparative gullibility of his fellow mirrors and commons, all of which fell once or twice most seasons. I had no doubt that this gorgeous fish was endowed with a little more cleverness than the ordinary carp.

My observations so close to home have been repeated again, once in a tiny carp syndicate water and again at the larger broad outside Norwich University. In both waters large and beautiful koi carp existed, fish that I quite set my heart upon for short, intensive, fruitless periods. I knew that they fed

Binoculars are essential to make out a fish at a distance.

on all the usual carp baits and I saw them do this on occasions, but getting them to accept one with a hook in it was a quite different affair. Indeed, in the small pool, just to see the koi was an achievement. There were only three of them and the largest was a quite spectacular ivory and lemon fish of some 15–17lb. I saw him just three times in a solid month – always moving very quickly as if almost perpetually disturbed. Perhaps, I wondered then, their glaring colours make the fish feel conspicuous and neurotic and wary of their very shadows. Later I saw some big kois in the massive ornamental pool of a friend. They were taking bread from the toes of his small children. He told me that they were tamed, easily, in a time far shorter than he knew for any other fish. Then I began to wonder if the koi is just blessed with more – let us not say intelligence, but mental ability of the fishy sort.

GOLDEN TENCH

Sadly, with this fascinating and beautiful fish, I have no record at all. My grandmother, in her courting days around the turn of the century, fished Woburn with her fiancé, the man who became my grandfather and who unfortunately died before I was born. Here there were golden tench, as stated by Buckland in his *Natural History of British Fishes*, and grandmother enthused me greatly with stories of the two and three pounders she and grandfather used to catch. As a result, when still only a child of five or six, I decided that the golden tench was a fish I would catch. I never have. Of course, golden tench are not indigenous to England and the stocks of the last century were brought in from Germany in the 1860s and have in all probability withered dramatically over the last few years. However, the trail is not utterly dead and I have had rather bad fortune. In 1975 I was fishing Lyng pit very hard for tench to 4lb, always expecting a large one. One morning, I decided on a sortie to the nearby Wensum. My former wife fished the pit as usual. The tench for some reason were going mad that day and she had twenty-six of them, including a golden tench. All were returned as she knew my abhorrence of keepnets, and all I have ever had to go on is her description of a wondrous glowing fish more butter-yellow than gold with occasional large black spots. Naturally, I fished the summer out at Lyng after that and equally inevitably saw nothing of this fabulous fish.

Undoubtedly, pockets of golden tench still do exist here and there. In fact, that master photographer Jim Tyree showed me a transparency of one quite recently – a sight that rekindled my desire for one after all these years of longing.

Summer joy.

FLOUNDER

Certainly the flounder can be classed as a freshwater fish for they are the only sea fish quite capable of adapting to a lifetime out of salt water. Indeed, in Holland this big flatfish even breeds in what was the Zuider Zee, the Ijsselmeer, which is now completely fresh.

Flounders are great river-travellers and I know Fred Buller has landed them 25 miles from salt water when roach fishing on the Tweed, in which river they ascend even as far as Kelso. I myself have had them on the Hampshire Avon when freelining worms for barbel. However, it is as a stillwater species that we must look at them and the best chances of contact are in the hundreds of miles of dykes, salty marshes and lagoons around the coastlines of Britain. Flounders are great explorers, and they will get into the unlikely pieces of water anywhere near the tideline.

But can flounders can ever be seen as worthy opponents? Although I confess I have not floundered for many years, my answer would be a definite yes.

The creek home of mullet and flounder.

Fishing for them is fun, they are interesting, sport can be brisk, they fight strongly and, I suppose, if you are inclined that way, they can well be eaten.

During the 1970s I fished for them a great deal, always in dykes and lagoons around the Norfolk and Suffolk coasts that were fresh enough to support roach, rudd, perch and bream, Flounders came along regularly and fought the best of all – and some, I confess, were eaten, grilled along with the excellent wild mushrooms that grew so prolifically around these waters. The species responded very well indeed to heavy baiting with maggots, accepting either the same bait or smallish worms on the hooks. Tackle, I found, had to be considerably lighter than the usual sea-fishing gear; in fact, most of my flounders fell to 2 or 3lb hooklengths to size 16 or 18 hooks. Bites were quite decisive and could easily be mistaken for a bream's. The fight, however, could not. A 2lb flounder would be everywhere in the drain, seemingly at once. They ran in short, juddering bursts and seemingly never tired until you got their heads up, and then they seemed instantly done for.

In truth, I doubt if I will ever flounder again myself. However, as I'd love a four-or even five pounder and as they do live in the most lovely lark-song-filled places – who can ever tell?

Summer fun.

GOLDEN ORFE

In 1981 I embarked upon a record orfe hunt on a small Norfolk lake containing four very big specimens, the largest two of which I guessed were six or more pounds. The lake beneath it held a larger stock of smaller orfe and even these fish of 8oz–2lb were extremely difficult to catch – a fact that should have given me a clue to the problems I would face from the pool of despair above.

In fact, I cracked even the smaller fish only a couple of times, both in periods of sultry, stormy weather when the shoals were up on the surface feeding and splashing in a highly agitated state. Then they could be caught at long range with a bubble float and a couple of maggots on a size 18 hook and very fine line. The fish I landed did not fight aggressively and were quite easily tamed on this gear.

Things were very different in the upper lake. Never once did I see those gigantic orfe feed on anything, even though I watched them constantly all summer through. That statement alone proves that I did not catch one or even register a bite. I used corn, maggots, brandlings, caterpillars, moths, grasshoppers, bread, artificial flies – just about everything known to anglers

– and never once did a mouth open or close with intent. Admittedly, the water was very rich in daphnia and the fish were absolutely indifferent to alien food supplies but, even so, those orfe showed an uncanny ability to keep up the barriers between man and fish.

Fortunately, this is not always the case in lakes everywhere and big orfe do get caught in those few waters where they have been stocked and thrive. Perhaps those men fortunate to have held these fish will agree with what I wrote upon holding my first three orfe:

All were, in the true sense, fabulous. From the dazzling shoulders the orange melted to salmon-tinged silver around the stomach and, even on that dull morning, they almost literally glittered. Then, almost with a shock, I realized that these orfe were roach! Or, at least, take their oriental colours away and they were. Shape, fins, eyes, mouths, scales – I checked each feature and but for the flood of colours there lay three prime roach.

MULLET

Grey mullet are, of course, sea fish by rights, but they do travel up rivers, infest coastal marshes and enter estuaries and lagoons, where the coarse angler can realistically get at them. Creek and sea mullet are virtually impossible to catch, in my experience, but those in the sluggish estuary pools are a different matter altogether. Here the mullet are less nomadic than their coast-roaming brothers and they will often sit tight from their first appearance around May or June until the onset of the winter pushes them south again around September. This stability is the key to catching them. The roaming fish remain totally wild and feed as nature intended them to, upon microscopic life in the algae-covered mud – food they scrape up with that hard-boned upper lip of theirs. No angler can hope to imitate such food and the shoals rarely stay around long enough for them to be weaned to an alien food supply.

Such is not the case with estuary and lagoon fish. Here, after a few weeks, the fish grow used to new types of nourishment and can be caught on an angler's tackle. Possibly there will be factories or warehouses around the estuary which disgorge waste material edible to the mullet. Certainly there will be lots of humans around working, or on leisure, and humans mean discarded food. Soon the mullet will learn that bread, cheese, pastry, cake and all manner of fruit and vegetables are tasty and nutritious. At once they become vulnerable.

Sunset over the marshes and the mullet that run with the tides.

John Judge and Joe Reed prepare a mullet swim – there will be water soon!

For four seasons I pursued mullet in the open creeks of the north Norfolk coast. In all that time I caught three fish – one on bread, one on a small ragworm and one on a tiny silver spoon. Then I discovered Gorleston harbour, where the Ross food factory washed waste peas and carrots down a pipe to the waiting mullet shoals. On my first visit I landed six and lost two. Tackle was exactly what I used for winter roaching on the Wensum. I took a risk in a way, for mullet do grow larger than roach and they fight at least a dozen times better. And they jump! The saving factor is, of course, that there are not as many snags in the sea and you can afford to let them go in most circumstances, though one big fish ran seventy yards to snag me fatally around an anchor chain.

Prebaiting definitely pays dividends in these circumstances. I generally use mashed bread flavoured with pilchard oil. The result is a soggy, smelly, colourful mess which draws mullet from a quarter of a mile away. There are very large mullet still to be caught in the semi-stillwaters around our coast. In many areas they tend to receive little attention and double-figure fish slip in and out of our waters all but unsuspected every summer.

Alternative Methods

Summer is the ideal time to play around with your fishing. Hot days, clear waters and long hours of daylight all encourage expansiveness, invention and enjoyment. Bobbing for eels or gudgeon on the Thames can simply be fun but some of the more unusual methods employed can be actually be useful fish-catching aids.

For example, I have only ever once fly-fished for carp. That was in the wake of an article on the subject by Chris Yates. My own attempt was a failure – though it might have been an outstanding and unlikely success. Simply, I had chanced upon a local carp lake in the heat of the afternoon when a great many fish were basking under the trees. The water was still with thick scum, with a large number of flies, mosquitoes and wasps trapped in it. One or two of these were taken in an idle sort of way by the carp and I saw enough to make me put a large artificial moth beneath the bubble float and fish that dry rather than the usual floater.

Alternative methods.

The classic shape of the wild carp – this one fell to the bait.

A smaller fish showed great interest in the fly and obviously wanted to take it. I, however, wished for a bigger fish and removed the moth from the carp's nose. That was my mistake; the fish bolted and took most of the shoal with it. Not since then have I really had the chance to test Chris's ideas out further. Recently, I heard that Norfolk angler Jim Tyree has had amazing successes fishing conventional floaters unconventionally on fly tackle. This is not my development, however, and it is up to Jim to say more if he wishes.

Nor have I personally any experience of fly fishing for tench, though I know a man who has. David Cooper is the long-standing bailiff at Blickling Lake – a notoriously hard tench water. The water here is generally very clear and is exceptionally rich in natural food. Tench are of course catchable on normal baits and methods but there are times that they seem totally preoccupied with tiny water insects and daphnia. It is at these times that David brings out the fly tackle that he wields with great skill. I gather he uses a very small nymph – something like a Pheasant Tail – tied on a size 16 hook or thereabouts and he twitches it back amongst feeding tench just above the bottom. Takes apparently are quite positive and he has no trouble hooking the tench responsible. One or two very good fish indeed have fallen to this method, which obviously does offer very real alternatives on certain types of lake.

David Cooper with a bait-caught tench this time.

On the same lake, a great many tench and bream typically escape to the shallows in the heat of the day. There they drift aimlessly in shoals or singly, taking little notice of anything and seemingly utterly uninterested in food. It is at such times that John Nunn in particular has done well by stalking them with light line, a small ledger weight and a long hooklength to a size 10 or so. He gets into the reeds with a jar of worms. As fish idle past him, he casts a worm a yard or so before them to sink slowly down in front of their noses. Then he watches either the worm or his line entering the water for a bite. The float, he rightly says, disturbs the fish in such shallow water. Not every cast by any means catches a fish and the method is hot and exhausting but when bites come they are positive and John gets some very good fish this way at a time when the rest of the lake is dozing.

When fish are in this kind of lazy mood the twitched bait can work well. A worm is the ideal bait, cast out and allowed to rest 30 seconds, then twitched

A magnificent late-summer tench carrying not a trace of spawn.

Roger Miller with another stalked, float-caught tench.

back 6 or 12 inches at a time with 20 seconds or so between each movement. An air-injected worm, or one held up by polystyrene, is often necessary to avoid the algae, weed and rubbish that collect on the beds of most summer stillwaters.

Heavily fished waters can get very difficult at this time of the year, especially when clarity and natural food stocks are at their height. Fine tackle, delicately presented baits and very restrained groundbaiting with the various aromatic mixes now on the market can still produce a fish or two. So can fishing tight against some distant island or major snag. However, the most predictable way to catch fish again is often to fish at night. Rudd, crucians and bream obviously respond to the darkness and so, dramatically, do stillwater roach. In the majority of waters I fish for good specimens, night is the only time they will feed between July and September and daytime sessions are pretty well a waste of time.

The twitched worm . . .

Summer night sessions can produce interesting side results. Years ago at Bayfield Lake, once night fell properly, 'clooping' started all along the wooded bank. The sucks and slobberings were of such magnitude that I realized carp had to be the culprits – even though I did not then know that they were present in the water. Out with my crust. The line tightened and I was into one of the very many tench I caught in this way. Since then, some of my best crucians and rudd have fallen in exactly the same way, except that baits and hooks were scaled down.

Fishing through summer nights often proves just how nocturnal pike can be at this time of year. Feeding sessions have often continued sporadically until dawn and probably every fish in the lake has attempted at least one meal. I mention this because a very well-respected piker told me recently that many of the hugely difficult Broadland waters responded far better in summer than they did in winter. He even went as far as hinting that if a really colossal pike were to fall again he expected it might well do so before September one year. Hearing this and knowing how active pike are on summer nights really made me think about a campaign for a serious fish. Of course, everyone knows now about the potential summer pike of floating plugs and the like, but this would be something rather different.

. . . pays off.

Summer roach are worth pursuing.

The crystal waters of Bayfield Lake.

Summer pike potential.

Summer perch are also generally overlooked. On a local lake, all through the summers of 1987, 1988 and 1989, shoal after shoal of small roach were hit day in and day out by perch shoals, often right in front of rows of anglers. Not one would make any effort to capitalize on these 2lb-plus fish, which were virtually shouting, 'Here I am. Catch me!' A twitched worm, a plug, a small dead roach from the margin would all have stood a chance of a beautiful fish and yet they were rarely, if ever, tried.

As a child, my favourite form of summer fishing was to use floating casters to attract the fish to the surface and then to catch them with a matchstick float, greased line and a size 20 buried deep in one of the rich bronze shells. The whole method was rather like fly fishing and I found it both exciting and productive. Since then I have found on occasion that it can be a useful way to tempt big fish. There are times when a shoal of good rudd, wild carp, roach or whatever will congregate in a quiet area and bask in or below the accumulations of scum. They will not look at bottom baits and conventional

A surface-caught rudd.

floaters are too large to interest them. Casters, though, being small and tasty, are frequently taken and often with gusto. A single caster on a size 16 to a double-strength 4lb hooklength will land most fish up to 3 or 5lb in weight – though one or two fish are likely to be the limit before the shoal breaks up and drifts away to quieter pastures.

Index